# PRAISE

## WHO YOU ARE

Who am I? It's an age-old question we all ask, a quest for which we all want an answer. In our modern world, we are told to look inside, search yourself, you be you—but Judy Cha knows better. In *Who You Are*, Judy points to the ancient Scriptures containing timeless truths about our God-given identity. Read her look into the biblical remedy to our contemporary ailment, and learn who you are.

—Kyle Idleman, bestselling author of *Not a Fan* and *When Your Way Isn't Working*

A timely invitation back to our identity in Christ in a cultural season that overemphasizes the therapeutic self apart from God. Judy Cha carefully acknowledges the multifaceted complexities of the soul from a biblical and psychological perspective, not shying away from the realities of our survival strategies that keep us stuck and provides a framework for internalizing the gospel. This was a refreshing read, and I highly recommend it for anyone hungry to remember who they are in light of the gospel.

—Colleen Ramser, licensed professional counselor, Colleen Ramser Counseling

*What is wrong with us?* I often have this thought when reading the news, playing sports, driving home, watching a movie, or even listening to my own family. Our world is broken, and I am part of the problem. In *Who You Are*, seasoned counselor Judy Cha reveals the real problem and unveils the ultimate solution. There is only one thing that can make us right—the gospel of Jesus Christ. Read this book and find out who you are.

—Caleb Kaltenbach, bestselling author of *Messy Grace* and *Messy Truth*

The work of Redeemer Counseling Center, spanning decades, has been a lifeline to thousands of New Yorkers experiencing the transformative power of the gospel. Under Judy Cha, the counseling center has grown to be an institution that is critical to the mission and health of gospel renewal in New York. Judy's leadership and work in the field has paved the way for gospel-centered clinical therapy in ways the Christian counseling world has long needed. This book not only unpacks gospel-centered clinical therapy but also beautifully weaves in Judy's personal narrative and her own work in fully experiencing her identity in Christ. The book is the culmination of the collective wisdom and research of Judy's counseling team and staff.

—MAI HARIU-POWELL, executive director, the
New York Project, Redeemer City to City

Wise, personal, and practical, Judy Cha's beautiful book will awaken you to an experience of God's love so you are freed from shame and empowered to live with greater wholeness, joy, and lightness of being.

—KEN SHIGEMATSU, pastor of Tenth Church,
Vancouver, and author of *Now I Become Myself*

Judy Cha's *Who You Are* will immediately strike a chord with you. Cha puts her finger on a timeless human problem we all struggle with: What is our identity? Cutting through the cultural noise with biblical precision and compassion, Cha helps us navigate biblically faithful ways to understand ourselves and our situation. Because of her long and deep service in the counseling community, I thought at first glance the book might be specifically for counselors and those we speak with, but after a thorough reading, I'm convinced this is a book every human being should read and take in.

—JONATHAN D. HOLMES, executive
director, Fieldstone Counseling

Using her personal experience and decades of work as a counselor, Judy Cha tells us how to find our true identity and greater intimacy with God. She shows us how to discover and gain freedom from our deep idols and how to be healed through the gospel of grace. She demonstrates how wholeness is found only in Christ as she reveals the hidden dangers found in our own self-defeating strategies. Cha is a wise and courageous guide who shows us that we can know who we are only in relationship with God and others and also shows us how we can give that gift to others.

—MICHELLE LEE-BARNEWALL, affiliate professor of New Testament at Talbot School of Theology, Biola University, and author of *A Longing to Belong*

If you think psychotherapy isn't deep enough or biblical counseling isn't helpful, this book is for you. Judy brings the best of both together to get to the heart of what needs to be fixed in our broken lives. The answer is wise and clinically researched and gives hope to all through a new identity in Christ.

Judy is an exceptional counselor, and this book shows why. Her wisdom, compassion, humility, and experience are found on every page. Her model developed at Redeemer Counseling over the past three decades combines the best of sound biblical theory and carefully researched therapy. The GIFT approach enables lasting change at every level of a person's identity in Christ.

—ANDREW FIELD, pastor, Redeemer Church West Side

This book is a journey that delves into the depth of who we are. It unravels the intricacies of our true identities while not missing the shaping influences we have had along the way. The book skillfully addresses core issues with biblical wisdom, equipping you to know and understand yourself while giving you a roadmap to true healing found in deeply connecting with God through your identity in Christ.

—ELIZA HUIE, LCPC, director of counseling at McLean Bible Church

Dr. Judy Cha's *Who You Are* is a most welcome contribution to a discussion that will only continue to intensify in importance—namely, "How do we minister the gospel effectively to individuals shaped by wounds incurred in an increasingly diverse and complex world?" For years Dr. Cha has led a group of New York City counselors who are astute to the insights of evidence-based psychotherapy but animated to the core by their love for Jesus Christ, their trust in his Word, and their conviction that his gospel is powerful to liberate, heal, and restore. In this volume she pulls back the curtain on their insights and methods. The included optional exercises give readers an opportunity to experience healing along the way.

—Dr. Jay Harvey, assistant professor of pastoral
theology and executive director, Reformed
Theological Seminary, New York City

*Who You Are* is a book for our times. Many are feeling the hopelessness of an unstable identity and a disconnection from God in an unstable world. Judy Cha guides us through today's difficult emotional terrain of countless "triggering" events and longing for a certainty that won't annihilate who we are. She does so using the timeless truths of God's Word, hard-won lessons of her immigrant experience as a child, many years of counseling experience and access to sound psychological and brain research. This book is jargon free. It echoes Tim Keller's grace-filled teaching. It can be understood by Christian and non-Christian alike.

I see now how my own lay counseling—and my self-counseling too!—have not gone to the root of the problems we all suffer from. For example, buried pain/shame coupled with Band-Aid solutions we reach for unconsciously. If you are willing to start the pathway Judy lays out, please do it! You will find the gospel of Christ moving from your head to your heart in transformative hope-filled ways. It will be worth every bit of your investment in yourself.

—Lourine A. Clark, executive coach
and management consultant

Identity formation is not just one of the "big issues" of our time, but because identity is, by implication, central to who we are, it is the lens through which we see all other issues. *Who You Are* is an outstanding book to help us navigate a way forward in this important and emotionally charged area. Judy Cha writes with a rare blend of gracious insight honed through 10,000 counselling sessions and gospel truth applied in an integrated and thoughtful way. She is particularly adept at giving tools to the reader to help bridge the stubborn gap between head and heart so that the gospel takes root in our identity. The book also makes important points for the church to engage with on the integration between body and mind in pastoral care, as well as the destructive nature of shame as a distinct corollary to guilt. Whether you are a counsellor seeking to develop in this vital area of identity or a layperson wanting to live free from shame, knowing more fully the grace of Jesus Christ, this book really is a must-read.

—PETE NICHOLAS, senior pastor, Redeemer
Presbyterian Church Downtown

For Christians seeking to understand the world around us and their own emotional struggles, this book is a gift. Dr. Cha takes complex psychological material and makes it accessible and compelling. She argues persuasively that theology matters in our lives and particularly in our experience with feelings, but she doesn't stop there. She goes on to demonstrate what can be done about it. This is a tool kit for spiritual and psychological growth. Dr. Cha offers her heart and her years of experience as a therapist listening to people's pain, distress, and self-shaming. She tackles the why of these common human dilemmas and presses on to offer a path toward healing and release in changing how we see God and God's redemption project, seeking to restore us to a relationship rooted not in our efforts to be successful, but in the wide expanse of God's love and grace. Take time to read this book slowly and thoughtfully. Allow Judy to help you see yourself and your world through a new lens.

—GWEN M. WHITE, PsyD, director, Circle Counseling,
Philadelphia, and professor emeritus, Eastern University

Shame tells a story about us: what we have done, what has been done to us, and who we are. The gospel also tells a story that covers our shame and gives us a new identity. *Who You Are* takes us through a biblical process of transformation grounded in decades of practice at Redeemer Counseling Services. I can tell you this approach of facing your pain and internalizing the gospel will require a lot of hard work, but it is filled with hope and healing that you may not even be able to imagine now. Therefore, I recommend the life-giving process this book offers to us.

—DR. BRUCE O'NEIL, pastor, Redeemer Church LSQ

Our perception of who we are and whose we are affects every area of our lives, both positively and negatively. This much-needed book will help you identify the why behind your struggles and how to move forward in truth and freedom.

—BEN BENNETT, author, content creator,
director of Resolution Movement

*who*
YOU
*are*

# who YOU are

## INTERNALIZING THE GOSPEL TO FIND YOUR TRUE IDENTITY

## JUDY CHA

ZONDERVAN
REFLECTIVE

ZONDERVAN REFLECTIVE

*Who You Are*
Copyright © 2023 by Judy Cha

Requests for information should be addressed to:
Zondervan, *3900 Sparks Dr. SE, Grand Rapids, Michigan 49546*

Zondervan titles may be purchased in bulk for educational, business, fundraising, or sales promotional use. For information, please email SpecialMarkets@Zondervan.com.

ISBN 978-0-310-15465-5 (audio)

Library of Congress Cataloging-in-Publication Data

Names: Cha, Judy, author.
Title: Who you are : internalizing the Gospel to find your true identity / Judy Cha.
Description: Grand Rapids : Zondervan, 2023.
Identifiers: LCCN 2023015854 (print) | LCCN 2023015855 (ebook) | ISBN
    9780310154631 (paperback) | ISBN 9780310154648 (ebook)
Subjects: LCSH: Identity (Psychology)—Religious aspects—Christianity.
    | Pastoral counseling. | Christian life. | Shame—Religious aspects—
    Christianity. | BISAC: RELIGION / Christian Ministry / Counseling &
    Recovery | PSYCHOLOGY / Psychotherapy / Counseling
Classification: LCC BV4509.5 .C424 2023  (print) | LCC BV4509.5  (ebook) |
    DDC 259/.1—dc23/eng/20230522
LC record available at https://lccn.loc.gov/2023015854
LC ebook record available at https://lccn.loc.gov/2023015855

Published in association with the literary agent Don Gates @ THE GATES GROUP.

Cover design: *Thinkpen Design*
Cover photo: © *La Gorda / Shutterstock*
Interior design: *Sara Colley*

Printed in the United States of America

23 24 25 26 27 28 29 30 31 32 /TRM/ 12 11 10 9 8 7 6 5 4 3 2 1

*To my parents, Sang Min and Young Sook Chang,*
*for loving me and showing me who Christ is!*

# CONTENTS

# INTRODUCTION

# OUR IDENTITY IN
# THE GOSPEL

For thirty years, I have journeyed with people through the difficult seasons in their lives. I have seen them face catastrophic losses, traumas, and addictions. I have had the privilege of witnessing remarkable courage and resilience in people as they persevere through unimaginable circumstances. At the same time, and more often than not, I have also witnessed brutal destruction and heartbreak, crippling people and keeping them stuck in the depths of their suffering. For many years, I have wondered, *What can relieve people in the midst of their torment and give them a greater sense of hope?*

In counseling we seek to understand and identify the underlying causes for a person's distress. After more than ten thousand counseling sessions, I have come to realize that at the core of most of these concerns is the problem of *identity*. And even further, I believe the problem of our identity is a *spiritual* problem.

When sin entered the world, humanity internalized shame. We are now born with an inherent sense of shame that forms the foundation for who we are. As a result, we are engaged in a quest to rectify the shame within us, often seeking to fix it on our own. Unfortunately, our efforts to fix our shame and obtain a stable identity inevitably fail. Why? Because who we are—our worth, purpose, and meaning in life—is only received in relationship to our Creator.

Our Creator's solution to our identity problem is not a structured method of redemption from shame, but a person—our Redeemer, Jesus Christ. When we engage in relationship with him and come to truly understand the gospel, God's message of grace through Christ, we are affirmed in our identity in Christ. When we receive our identity from God, that inner struggle against our internalized shame is relieved. The external crisis, no matter how devastating or frightening, can rage on, because knowing *who we are* will empower us to face whatever challenges come our way. Having said that, knowing who we are is not something that we can live out easily or constantly. It is a process of gradually working in and internalizing who *God* says we are by identifying and removing the barriers that keep us from fully living out who we are.

Over several decades of counseling, I've observed that simply knowing the solution to the problem of identity does not immediately translate to resolving the problem. The reality is that we face insurmountable obstacles to obtaining a stable identity. We live in a broken world, regularly experiencing the effects of sin. Moreover, we ourselves are infected with sin in body and soul, and this obstructs our own way to freedom from our perpetual quest for identity and resting in Christ. Yes, the problem of identity is ultimately a spiritual problem, but helping people receive and internalize what God says about them takes intentional effort. We must walk alongside them as they uncover wounds and detangle beliefs, gradually reversing the curse of the fall through the process of internalizing the gospel.

For more than twenty years, our team at Redeemer Counseling has worked to identify ways to make the gospel more real in people's lives. We've learned that the first step toward that goal is to define the problem thoroughly and comprehensively. We've observed that every counseling approach presents a theory of what is wrong with us, the central "pathology" that is at the root of dysfunctional and destructive behaviors. To "fix" anything, we first need to know what is broken. Although our physical and psychological brokenness are readily acknowledged in counseling practice today, our spiritual brokenness is often overlooked, or at least is not taken seriously enough. So our aim is to bring the best of biblical and clinical insights to the practice of counseling. As a result, we developed a framework we call the Gospel-Centered Integrative Framework for Therapy (GIFT). This framework provides a way of defining what is wrong and shows how we can contextualize the solution to best help people experience the gospel and lasting heart change.

In the GIFT, it is recognized that to make sense of what

is wrong and what can help us, we need to pay close attention and be curious about our own life stories. Everybody has a story, a context of how we came to be who we are today. Our stories introduce us to important characters who have influenced us, key events that elated us, and those that harmed us. It includes critical moments in our history that shaped our dreams, set our course of direction in life, and transformed our relationships. There is so much to our life stories! In all my years of working with people, I've never heard stories that are exactly the same, and I've never heard a story that didn't intrigue me—including my own. Our stories are made up of unique experiences that shape and influence who we are in the present. The uniqueness of our stories is not only what we've experienced but, more importantly, how we've made sense of our experiences. In each of our stories, we see how our identity—our sense of self and self-worth—is shaped and reinforced. By better understanding our stories, we can work toward removing the barriers to obtaining our true and stable identity.

I am convinced that our best hope for addressing our real problem, the problem that underlies such things as our self-doubt, our loneliness, our broken relationships, and our lack of faith, lies in obtaining a stable identity as we internalize the gospel. Throughout this book, I share some of my own story as well as composite stories from my counseling experience to illustrate the concepts and processes I address. This book begins by looking at *what is wrong with us*, the obstacles that lie in the way of understanding our true identity. In part 2, I describe *what can make us right*, the gospel that is progressively internalized. Then, in part 3,

I explain how we can *internalize the gospel*, and I suggest a few practical ways to do that.

At the end of each chapter, I invite you to take time to reflect on how to better understand your own life story. You can use these reflections on your own to journal or take notes about what is coming up for you as you reflect, or use them with a group as you process with trusted friends who are also reading the book. My hope is that by engaging in this process of reflecting, you will discover more about who you are.

PART ONE

# WHAT IS WRONG WITH US?

# ONE

# THE REAL PROBLEM AND THE ULTIMATE SOLUTION

My journey as a counselor began at a rehabilitation center for patients with severe head traumas, most of whom had been involved in serious car accidents. Several had experienced injuries that limited their physical mobility and mental functioning. However, their longing for connection, a sense that they were known and accepted by another, was very evident. Even though I was only a patient care coordinator, a few patients and coworkers called on me to help restore a sense of calm in some distressing situations. This happened enough times that in one staff meeting I was asked why this certain patient, known for his angry outbursts and resistance toward everyone, would respond only to me. As a twenty-four-year-old recent seminary graduate, I had learned and believed that God's love is so great that it is irresistible and ultimately the answer to everything. So I remember saying something like, "He feels God's love through me!" My colleagues' reaction wasn't memorable enough for me to recall, but I remember feeling like I was the odd one out in the group. Eventually I left this job and joined my husband, who was a pastor, in ministry.

Being confident in the gospel and feeling well-equipped to help people change, I entered ministry with a great deal of optimism. Looking back now, I realize how much I grossly underestimated how complex people are and the mess sin has caused in us and around us. Even now, thirty years later, I confess I've never felt as confident as I did then about my readiness for ministry, but I have remained confident about one thing—the gospel. The gospel is the redemptive power of Christ to heal and change lives, and this is particularly true in the context of counseling. I've spent most of my career exploring how counselors can help people experience gospel healing and change through the practice of counseling.

One critical aspect of effective counseling is our ability to make sense of the problem, or the underlying issue, as we commonly call it. When we don't have a good way of making sense of the real problem underneath the surface problem, our solutions will inevitably be superficial, incomplete, or altogether irrelevant. Unfortunately, as a young counselor, even though I was certain about the gospel as the ultimate solution to people's problems, I had a very limited view of how to make sense of the real, underlying problem.

I grew up in the church and was trained at seminary, so my lens for defining the underlying problem landed on one of the following four assumptions:

1. **THE PROBLEM IS PERSONAL SIN.** I thought there were plenty of scriptures to support this premise, including Isaiah 53:6 and Romans 3:23. I particularly liked Jeremiah 17:9, which says, "The heart is deceitful above all things and beyond cure." The problem is our unconfessed, hidden sin. The aim in counseling is to help people see what they are not seeing or expose what they are hiding, and then help them repent.

2. **THE PROBLEM IS SPIRITUAL WEAKNESS.** People struggle because they don't know better. They are spiritually immature (1 Cor. 3: 1–4; Eph. 4:14; Heb. 5:11–14). My goal was to help them grow. They need to learn to feed on the Word and know more of God's truth. So I should tell them what they need to know— God's truth.

3. **THE PROBLEM IS WOUNDEDNESS.** The Bible tells us we will have trouble in this world and to expect suffering (John 16:33; Rom. 8:18; 1 Peter 4:12). The book of Psalms seems to validate our pain and suffering. So people need to face their wounds. They need to forgive, pray, and ask for and receive God's healing.

4. **THE PROBLEM IS SPIRITUAL WARFARE.** As 1 Peter 5:8 says, the devil prowls around like a roaring lion, seeking someone to devour. People are under attack, and they are trapped in their sin patterns. This interferes with their healing and growth. They need deliverance prayer to bind the workings of the devil.

My favorite go-to was number 1, the problem of personal sin. After all, you can't go wrong with this diagnosis, since we all are sinners! However, as I began to gain more experience and saw more and more people, I realized that focusing on any one of these four as the core problem was far too simplistic. Personal sin, spiritual weakness, woundedness, and spiritual warfare alone could not account for what I was seeing in my meetings with Lindsey, the grieving mom who lost her only son to cancer; Bill, the young pastor who contracted a mystery sickness that flattened him physically and led to his termination; Cathy, the college student who was binging and purging daily as a way to manage her stress; and Doug, a young father, who despite his efforts to be sober, relapsed again and again. The problems people were presenting had multiple root causes and varied symptoms that were hard to understand and treat. Over time it became clear to me that the problem is all of these, *and* most likely much more. I was beginning to see how when sin entered our world, it didn't just affect individuals; sin tainted all of creation and made us even more vulnerable physically, emotionally, and spiritually. So the question I was facing was how to make *better* sense of the problem so I could help people *better* experience God's healing and his power to change lives.

The solution did not come immediately. In fact, it took more than a decade of working with people and consulting with other counselors to develop a framework for comprehensively identifying the problem. In this chapter, I provide you with an overview of how to make sense of the problem that perpetuates our identity crisis, how the gospel is the solution that can fix the problem, and what processes are needed to internalize the gospel and address the real problem. In later chapters, we'll get into more of the details of how this problem develops and how we can obtain a stable identity.

## OUR SYSTEM OF SELF-REDEMPTION

It's easy to say we believe in God and what the Bible says about who we are. Yet we have such a hard time relinquishing our reliance on ourselves! We continue to assert who we are and hide parts of ourselves. Self-help resources and books, which aim to help individuals *independently* improve some or all aspects of their lives, have gained popularity in the last decade as we've become more and more individualistic as a society. The demand for these self-help resources isn't hard to understand. Life can be perplexing and beset with obstacles, yet life also presents us with a myriad of possibilities. People are hungry for guidance to overcome life's challenges and seize the opportunities to become the best human beings possible. In the counseling world, we call this the process of self-actualization, in which we progressively reach our full potential. This observation reveals a fundamental trait common to all humanity—we rely on ourselves to fix what we think is wrong with us.

In many instances, this reliance on ourselves, our ability to use our human agency to resolve problems and fulfill our desires, can be a sign of health and maturity. In our culture, our sense of who we are and our value are closely bound to our abilities and achievements. Human agency refers to our capability to influence our world and the course of events by our actions. We form intentions, action plans, and strategies toward realizing what we aim for. We also have the ability to regulate and control our thoughts, motivations, and behaviors through the influence of our belief systems. This capacity to exercise control over our internal processes to set us on a course of action is a distinctively human characteristic, a quality that I believe is God-given, and a way we bear God's image.

Yet although our agency is to be celebrated, we often forget that our agency is limited. We are created beings, and when we solely depend on our agency to live life, to save us from hardship, and to give us an acceptable identity, then God is no longer God. God becomes irrelevant to us. We replace him with another god over our lives. The self becomes an idol. Thus, our problem begins with our innate propensity toward the idol of self by creating our own *system of self-redemption* (SOSR).

The SOSR is a system within us that forms in the context of our personal narratives. We develop this internal system to redeem our shame and validate our identity, purpose, and worth apart from God. Ever since the fall, our spiritual reality is that we are disconnected from God, the one from whom we are meant to derive our identity, and therefore we experience shame. To remedy this, we turn to the self to save ourselves and to remove the sense that something is wrong with us. However, as derived identities we also make meaning of our experiences in this fallen world. We make subjective interpretations of our shame and develop strategies to make right what is wrong. In other words, our propensity for self-redemption is within us from the time we are born, but the aspects that make up our own SOSR are uniquely shaped by our life stories. The SOSR is the way we capture the impact of sin comprehensively. Each component of the SOSR depicts an aspect of what is wrong with us.

At the core of the SOSR is the innate shame that is internalized in all of us as the result of being born as sinners. This shame-based identity is the basis for our *view of self* and motivates us to create our SOSR. All of us experience *core hurts*, our own experiences of pain and suffering that reinforce our shame and personalize the shame messages. For example, someone who was abused as a child may have experienced feeling used and devalued. These repeated experiences of wounding personalize the shame-based message *I am worthless* or *I am damaged*.

In the context of our pain, we also develop *idolatrous strategies* to avoid or suppress the pain and to assert an identity we deem as worthy. Unfortunately, our strategies are not always effective. So, when we face situations in which our strategies fail, we experience painful *reactive emotions*, which lead us to act immediately with *behavioral responses* to numb, distract, and alleviate the pain. What often brings people to counseling are the difficult present circumstances, the painful reactive emotions, and unhelpful behavioral responses. However, the deeper, underlying problems of shame, core hurts, and idolatrous strategies are frequently unnoticed by them.

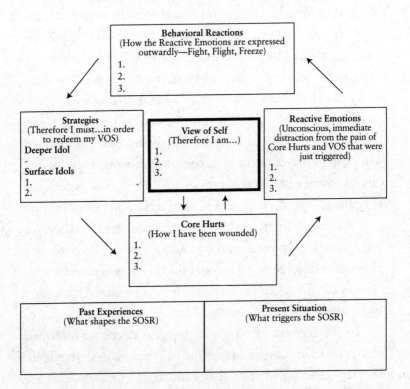

## SYSTEM OF SELF-REDEMPTION
(What do I need to do to feel okay about myself?)

**Behavioral Reactions**
(How the Reactive Emotions are expressed outwardly—Fight, Flight, Freeze)
1.
2.
3.

**Strategies**
(Therefore I must...in order to redeem my VOS)
Deeper Idol
-
Surface Idols
1.
2.

**View of Self**
(Therefore I am...)
1.
2.
3.

**Reactive Emotions**
(Unconscious, immediate distraction from the pain of Core Hurts and VOS that were just triggered)
1.
2.
3.

**Core Hurts**
(How I have been wounded)
1.
2.
3.

**Past Experiences**
(What shapes the SOSR)

**Present Situation**
(What triggers the SOSR)

Our SOSR should always be understood in the *context* of our life stories. Let's look at a case study of someone I'll call Emily, who represents a composite of clients we have seen at Redeemer Counseling.

From the time Emily enters the world, she has a sense that there is something wrong with the world and that she falls short of some standard of perfection. A quest for a system of self-redemption unfolds for measuring up and making sense of her world. This quest is shaped not only by her genetic disposition but also by her environment. As a small child, she begins to develop a sense of self and of others, especially based on her relationship with her parents, which invariably shapes her sense of God, however subconscious. Since she is by nature a derived identity, these early interpersonal encounters shape who she is and her sense of worth. This sets the foundation for her view of others and of God, as well as her interpretation of life experiences. As she makes sense of her joys, successes, losses, traumas, and social struggles, she begins to form deeply embedded views about how to make sense of her world, why things are broken, and how to make things right. Throughout her development, as she encounters more experiences and relationships, these views are expanded, reinforced, and altered.

We'll hear more about Emily and her SOSR in the chapters to come. What is important for us to understand now is that inevitably our quest to save ourselves ultimately leads to failure. Regardless of how hard we strive to justify ourselves through our SOSR, it only disappoints and enslaves us. Because we were created as dependent beings, we cannot redeem what is broken in us or justify ourselves to earn an identity. We need a Redeemer who will *give* us an identity.

## THE ULTIMATE SOLUTION
## IN THE GOSPEL

If the root pathology we face is a system of *self*-redemption, which ultimately is created due to our lost identity, then we need a redemptive power outside of ourselves to cover our shame and give us our sense of self and worth. This is what we have in the gospel of Jesus Christ. It is a story of his grace in which we receive an unmerited gift that has the power to heal and transform us. The gospel is about grace from beginning to end. In it we have a Redeemer who does not wait for us to get things right and pursue him. He comes to us and *makes* things right for us on the cross. He atones for our sins and establishes our new and absolute identity as heirs of God and fellow heirs with Christ (Rom. 8:17).

Not only is this grace the basis of our salvation, but it is the power for our sanctification. By grace we experience the reality that God accepts us as we are, walks with us through every step of the journey toward healing, and empowers us to grow and change. Only an encounter with such radical grace can produce both inward refining of character and outward service to others. In the gospel, we are not given a *system* for redemption—we are given a *person*, a Redeemer. When the gospel becomes progressively internalized and our relationship with Christ becomes more personal, we increasingly turn away from self-reliance and turn toward God, relying on his grace. Internalizing the gospel leads us to progressively relinquish our SOSR and experience the Spirit correcting our view of ourselves and our world. Just as our SOSR touches on all of the multifaceted ways we experience sin, the gospel can heal every aspect of sin, from individual to relational to systemic.

## INTERNALIZING THE GOSPEL

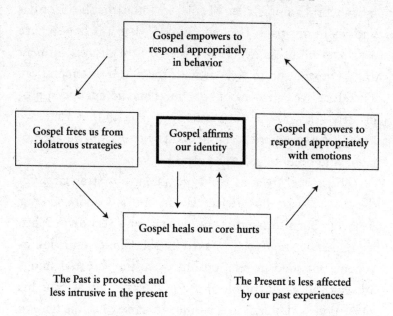

© 2006 Copyright of Redeemer Counseling Services

Since the gospel reconciles us to God, we are able to face him, and he becomes our source of derived identity. As a result, our view of self is progressively transformed as we internalize who God says we are. We are, in fact, not afraid to see our brokenness because we also see who we are in Christ and all he has done for us. That is, we can embrace that "we are more sinful and flawed in ourselves than we ever dared believe, yet at the very same time we are more loved and accepted in Jesus Christ than we ever dared hope."[1] We can simultaneously rejoice in our new identity and continue to repent of our wayward hearts.

The gospel heals our deepest *core hurts*. When we see Christ as the Suffering Servant who experienced life in a fallen world among fallen people, we know that he identifies with us in our pain. He understands what it is like to have a broken body, to experience the pain of disappointment and betrayal, and to wrestle with the allure of temptation. Therefore, we can face our core hurts and accept and appropriately grieve them. No matter how painful they were, we know Christ experiences our pain with us, so we are not alone and do not need to be afraid.

The gospel frees us from our idolatrous strategies. On the cross, Christ, our perfect Savior, not only addressed our depravity but also asserted our dignity as his very own. When we remember that we are saved by sheer grace, our desires become satisfied in relationship with him, created things are enjoyed as intended, and our motivations are for his glory alone. Although we continue to experience the tension between self-reliance and trusting in Christ, the grip of idolatry loses its power, and our strategies to redeem ourselves are progressively relinquished. We can thoroughly repent and wholeheartedly rejoice at the same time because of the gospel.

Lastly, the gospel empowers us to respond appropriately. We learn to validate our reactive emotions as God-given windows through which we can examine our hearts. We process emotions rather than being controlled by them. Our emotions become more appropriate to the context and do not overwhelm us with their intensity, allowing us to express them more wisely. Likewise, our *behavioral reactions* correspond with the challenges of the situations we encounter without the burden of our past hurts or the shame of our fallenness. Christ our Shepherd shapes us anew into people who progressively reflect and represent him and who display the fruit of the Spirit: love, joy, peace, patience, kindness, goodness, faithfulness, gentleness, and self-control (Gal. 5:22–23).

The gospel is more than a set of beliefs; it is a relationship with a living God, our Redeemer. When Christ becomes a real person in our lives as we internalize the gospel, our preoccupation with ourselves and our subsequent striving for an identity will gradually diminish.

## THE PROCESS OF HEALING AND CHANGE

As I reflect back to my first job as a patient care coordinator, I realize that my twenty-four-year-old self was right. The unruly, impulsive, angry patient did experience God's love through me. Jake was only eighteen years old when his car collided with an eighteen-wheeler truck. His injuries were so severe that he was in a coma for several months. He was tall, lean, and good-looking, though his face was noticeably scarred, either from the accident or the surgery—I didn't ask.

His head trauma had damaged his brain, especially the part that regulated his emotions. He told me that he had dreamed of becoming a professional baseball player. He was proud of his abilities and had many options to attend college on scholarships. But with one mistake his life was over. Now he was in despair, experiencing the inconsolable pain that came from losing his ultimate dream. Listening to his story, I felt heartbroken for him. He was only in his teens, far too young to feel as if his life was over. I felt for him—and he felt what I felt for him. That was the connection. I was there with him in his despair. I saw him, felt his despair, and was with him in it. He felt known and accepted by me.

And that is what Jesus did for us! He saw our predicament, felt our pain, and came in a physical body not only to be with us in all of this but to give his life for us. He wore the crown of thorns, was whipped and ridiculed, and he died to set us free from our pain forever. He sees us. He knows us. He completely accepts us. This is unmerited grace! And this longing to be known and accepted is not just appealing to those who have been injured, disabled, and marginalized. This longing that accompanies our internalized shame is within all of us.

Given how much we depend on and value our agency, imagine with me what it must be like for a person to admit they have made a mistake, they have sinned, they have been victimized, and they were and still are weak and relapsing week after week. I can imagine their shame-based identity raging against such admission and urging them to keep silent. This is the internal battle we must overcome, confess, and repent of. When we really know and experience God's love and acceptance of us—when we internalize the gospel—we can surrender our SOSR, own what is broken in us, yet feel secure in who we are. When our longing is fulfilled in God, our identity is affirmed, and we will not be afraid to face our sins, our hurts, or our shame.

So how do we internalize the gospel? The process is not an easy one, and it's typically not fast either. Certainly the process requires more on our part than just telling people about God or giving them Bible verses, and it has a lot to do with how the human brain works in making sense of God. We believe in a living God with whom we can have a real relationship, but he is not a physical being that we can experience through our human senses. So we use our imagination and form mental representations of God that resemble how we see people we are close to. This is part of the reason why we experience a gap between our head and heart knowledge of God and why we often hear people say, "I know the Bible says God loves me, but I don't feel it."

Take Jake, the young man in the eighteen-wheeler accident, for example. Let's say that he internalized the shame-based message that he is damaged and inadequate and sees others as disapproving and uncaring. These beliefs automatically and unconsciously will serve as a template to make sense of God too. Reading a text like "Do not be anxious about anything" (Phil. 4:6) will have a tone that Jake will hear as condemning and accusing, like he is doing something wrong by being anxious. He can hear sermons, attend Bible studies, and read Scripture, but when his unconscious beliefs about God do not match what he hears or reads, it's hard for him to take it in and make it real for him. So how do we close this gap between the head and heart knowledge of God? My dissertation study conducted at Redeemer Counseling confirmed that the most essential element in closing this gap is the corrective relational experiences that happen in human relationships.[2]

When Jake would act out, most of the staff reacted with exasperation and annoyance, leaving him alone in his room behind closed doors. On the other hand, my simple questions—"Are you okay, Jake?" and "Can I open the door?"—were relational experiences that were unexpected. This was a new relational experience for Jake, one in which he felt seen. My questions communicated to him that he was not alone in his pain, and this corrective experience contradicted his unconscious beliefs about himself and others. If these new relational experiences could be repeated over and over again, Jake's beliefs about God would also begin to shift.

It is pretty well established in the world of counseling that approximately 70 percent of favorable outcomes in counseling are attributed to the therapeutic relationship. Almost every model regards the strength of the therapeutic relationship as a key component in effective treatment. This means human relationships play a critical role in the healing process and in helping people internalize the gospel. This is so because we are not exactly like God even though we are made in his image. We have a physical body to experience life and form relationships. We are affected by what we experience in this physical world, both good and bad. Because our shame, the effects of our painful wounds, and the strategies we develop to protect ourselves and secure an identity operate in the unconscious mind, we need safe, warm, accepting, nonjudgmental relationships to explore the depth of our brokenness. When we feel safe, we are more willing to show our deepest vulnerabilities, like Jake did with me. He was able to share his despair, but not in an explosive way, and my presence was comforting to him even though I was not able to do anything to change his situation or solve his problems.

It makes even more sense to me now why we learn in Scripture that the greatest commandments are to love the Lord our God with all our hearts and with all our souls and with all our minds, and to love our neighbors as ourselves (Matt. 22:37–40). Loving God is connected to loving others. We need safe, meaningful relationships in which we experience the love of Christ to press into our identity in him. Every encounter we have with people is an opportunity to transform their perceptions of God and internalize the gospel. When they hear that God loves them, it will make better sense to them because they've experienced that through us.

## *Reflection*

Consider your present struggle. Perhaps you struggle with a difficult relationship with someone you love, or difficulty regulating your emotions, like anxiety or anger. Perhaps you are feeling hopeless, unable to break free from an ongoing behavioral pattern. Write out your response to the following questions.

1. What are you struggling with in the present?
2. How have you made sense of your struggle?
3. What have you tried to overcome your struggle?

# TWO

# OUR LOST IDENTITY
# AND THE EXPERIENCE
# OF SHAME

All of us, at one time or another, have experienced a sense that there is something wrong with us. It's a state of being that says something like, *I am not good enough; I am worthless; I am a mistake*; or *I don't deserve to exist*. Even though we don't walk around under the weight of this state all the time, this sense that something is wrong with us cannot be avoided. The reality is that we have conversations inside ourselves and with ourselves much of the day, some of which we are aware of and some not so much. However, the chatter inside of us gets louder and harsher when one of these states of being gets provoked.

The other day, as I was consulting with my supervisor,

he pointed out what I perceived to be a rookie mistake as a counselor. At the moment, I felt embarrassed, but I noticed that throughout the day my mind kept replaying this moment, causing me to feel less and less competent as a counselor. When I turned my attention to my inner dialogue, it went something like this: *Wow . . . how in the world did you miss that? You've been counseling for how many years now? You really should have known better. Maybe you shouldn't see people until you get some more training. It's really embarrassing and disappointing that you would miss something like that. I can't believe you're such an idiot!* The interaction with my supervisor provoked the sense that I'm not good enough and made me feel incompetent as a counselor. And I was preoccupied with being critical of myself for a good portion of the day.

Why does this happen? Why are we so susceptible to the message that something is wrong with us? The short answer is that we all experience this because we are born with internalized shame that's constantly operating underneath our conscious awareness. Our inner state of being is one of shame. This internalized shame is a spiritual reality that we have inherited from our first parents, Adam and Eve (Gen. 3:7–8). As a result of this deep sense of shame within, our past experiences of shame stick with us much more easily and color our interpretations of what happens to us and around us.

When I was eight years old, my family moved to America from Korea. At the time, there were very few kids like me in my school, and I was bullied and treated like an outsider. These repeated experiences of feeling humiliated and discarded as a child personalized and reinforced the innate shame that was already a part of me. This voice says I'm not good enough, I'm defective, and I'm worthless. In the context of my painful past, I developed a strategy to work hard and be as perfect as I could be to avoid feeling humiliated and to assert an identity that I am good enough. That strategy is still deeply embedded inside me. It says that who I am in my career as a counselor is more important to my identity and value than who God says I am. In this latest incident with my supervisor, my feelings of incompetence indicated that my strategy had failed. So, when my shame gets provoked, often unexpectedly, I feel ashamed and frustrated with myself, and I react by being critical of myself and self-condemning.

I believe our shame is rooted in our spiritual condition, so to understand why this happens to all of us, we have to go back to our origins and consider how we were made. In this chapter, we will explore the origins of our shame and its grip on who we are, how shame gets personalized in our stories, and how shame gets reinforced and passed on through learned relationship patterns.

## THE ORIGIN OF SHAME AND ITS GRIP

Often when people seek counseling, they present crippling symptoms of depression or anxiety, a variety of addictive behaviors, or devastating losses or traumas. Rarely does anyone come into my office asking for help to overcome their shame, and if they do, it is usually about getting over feeling humiliated or ashamed as a result of a recent incident or a memory of a past experience. However, the problem of shame is now accepted by both Christian and secular clinicians as the root problem behind most, if not all, of people's presenting concerns.

Shame is the problem behind every problem, and the origin of our shame is not limited to our dysfunctional families or to any hurtful experiences we've faced in our developmental history. The problem of shame is a spiritual one, and it is connected to how we are made. In Genesis 1:26–28, we read that we were made in the image of God. As image bearers, we were designed to know *who we are*—our value, purpose, and meaning in life—in relationship with God. We are created to derive our identity from God, which means that our sense of self and worth cannot be generated within ourselves but can only be received from God. Therefore, the problem of shame began when sin separated us from God, our Creator, from whom we are to derive our identity. I've often referred to the problem of shame as the universal pathology of all humanity. Shame is much more than a feeling. It is a sense of being, an intrinsic nature that operates beneath our awareness, but is so deeply internalized that we cannot escape it. Shame is what permeates our identity since the fall.

Even though we have internalized shame as a result of losing connection with our primary source of identity, our innate nature to derive our identity from outside of ourselves still remains. There are at least two implications for what it means to be created as *derived identities*. First, we are made to experience perfect intimacy with God and one another—the experience of being fully known and unashamed (Gen. 2:25). Second, we are made to receive information from outside of ourselves and make sense of what we receive. God told Adam and Eve not only who they were, but what they should do and how they should live (Gen. 1:28). These implications tell us that we are relational beings who are made to know and be known in close relationships with others, and that these relationships will have a profound impact on us. It is also implied that we are social beings who not only learn about ourselves through other people's responses to us, but we also shape our norms based on sources outside of us, such as social networks, religious affiliations, and our culture.

Because we long for acceptance from others and depend on outside information to define our identity, we are highly susceptible to messages from others as well as our culture about who we are and who we should be. It was important for me, growing up as a minority, to be accepted into mainstream Western culture. Within days of arriving in the United States, I was given an English name and encouraged throughout my formative years to shed any resemblance to my native culture and assimilate into the dominant culture. I tried to speak English without an accent and learn the mannerisms and fashion trends of American culture. As I think about my experience now, I see that this social pressure to assimilate actually did more harm than good to my identity formation. As much as I tried to assimilate into the dominant culture, I didn't quite fit in, which reinforced the message that I was not good enough.

When shame is provoked, it is agonizing because it reminds us of what we lost in the garden—that experience of being known and unashamed. In our present reality, we long to be known and accepted, but deep down, shame says that we are not acceptable. Shame is not only an indication of our fallen state, but shame is what drives our obsession to seek an identity that we deem acceptable and to assert our value. The more we experience shame, the more we will seek to assert an identity that is acceptable or withdraw and isolate in an effort to hide who we are. By doing so, we hope to negate or suppress our shame. Unfortunately, our efforts will not save us. Shame will be provoked again and again. We will not be set free from the experience of shame until all of creation is fully restored according to God's redemptive plan.

The quest for an identity has been around as long as we have existed, but in recent decades it has become more difficult for us, especially in Western culture, to obtain a stable sense of who we are. The resounding message in our culture is that no one else should have any say about who we really are, but instead, that each of us should have the autonomy and authority to define and assert our own identity. While our culture promotes this ever-intensifying focus on the individual and our agency to define ourselves, the creation narrative in Genesis suggests a far different way of knowing who we are. Because we are made to derive our identity from God, we cannot find ourselves within ourselves. Rather, the more we deepen our connection with God and the more he becomes our supreme validator, the more stable our identity will be and the more we will be set free from our shame.

## PERSONALIZED SHAME
## IN OUR LIFE STORIES

Our separation from God is the root cause of our shame, but shame becomes personalized to each of us as we live our lives. As I've alluded to in my own story, we all have a story of how we've become who we are.

Let's continue with the story of Emily, a thirty-two-year-old single woman in New York City who has recently had a string of misfortunes. Emily came to see me after months of trying to regain her ability to function. She was struggling to even get herself out of bed each day in time for our scheduled counseling meeting. After eight months of working at a multinational company as the communications director, she was terminated. Devastated by this loss but too ashamed to ask for help, she did what she usually does—strive to fix the problem. She tried and tried to find another job without success for more than six months. To make matters worse, the man she thought she would marry, the one she left her home, family, and career in North Carolina for, ended the relationship. Despite being a committed Christian, well-educated, and hardworking, she was now feeling unseen, afraid, and alone.

Emily's experience of feeling unseen, afraid, and alone is not a new experience for her. In fact, it can be traced back to her early childhood. Emily was the oldest of three children. Her parents married young at the age of twenty-two. Coming from a detached family, her dad longed for connection, while her mom, coming from an unstable family riddled with emotional distresses and financial woes, longed for a sense of security. But neither of them could provide what the other really needed. In the midst of heightened tensions and conflicts in their marriage, Emily was born.

For as long as she can remember, Emily felt like she was constantly on the edge. Sensing the tension between her parents, she waited in fear for the eruption of a conflict, which was terrifying for a young child. Emily knew that her parents were not available to help her with her fears. In fact, they were too preoccupied to even notice that she was scared. Even though she was too young to name what she felt in these moments, she experienced feeling unseen, afraid, and alone. These repeated experiences then led to the internalized message that she didn't matter, was not important, and was not worthy of being cared for.

Emily's job loss and rejection by her boyfriend triggered the shame that had been personalized in her relationships with her parents. As mentioned, our nature is to derive our identity from what someone outside of us says about us. We continue to look for something to image, someone outside of ourselves to define who we are and affirm our value. Emily, like all of us, was born with a longing for connection to a source of her identity, and her parents, as her early caregivers, were the first "mirrors" from which she learned to see herself. This is why our early experiences with our parents or caregivers have such lasting effects on us.

Our internalized shame is pervasive even though we do not live in constant awareness of it or feel oppressed by it. Shame is embedded in our unconsciousness, influencing how we think and how we make sense of our experiences.

It governs what we feel and moves us to act and react to our environment. Shame can even be contained in our bodies. It is behind our every struggle. When Emily lost her job, her shame was triggered, and it said, *You are not good enough.* Then her anxiety spiked, and her immediate response was to look for another job, hoping that getting another job would alleviate her shame. When our shame is provoked and our strategies to abate it do not work, shame erodes away our hope and pushes us to the point of despair. Emily felt devastated by the pain of the rejection by her boss and her boyfriend, but she could not reach out to anyone. These experiences provoked her shame, but her shame also kept her isolated, and eventually shame left her paralyzed and stuck.

Because shame cannot be avoided, we are more sensitive to the messages that fit what is deeply embedded and innate in us. The experiences and messages that correlate to the internalized sense that something is wrong with us have a firmer grip on who we are than those that communicate the opposite. This is why the experiences of being criticized or the message that *I am bad* sticks to us more than a compliment that conveys, *I am good.* John Gottman, relationship expert and researcher, once noted that five positive interactions are needed to neutralize the effects of one negative interaction. He coined it as the magic ratio of 5:1.[1] A shame-based message about ourselves needs five affirming messages to offset its effects.

As a child, Emily could not hold back her tears as tensions would build between her parents. Unfortunately, her fears were never acknowledged by either of her parents. Her dad would raise his voice and yell, "Stop crying!" Emily was never sure if her dad really liked her. He had a stern look about him—furrowed brows, curled lips, and a clenched jaw. Often when he looked at her, she felt like he was glaring or displeased with her. She doesn't remember any moments of physical warmth. At times he seemed interested in what she was doing and even told Emily that he was proud of her, but these comments didn't land for Emily. Even in those moments, she didn't feel that he was *truly* pleased with her. Emily's interactions with her mom weren't any more positive. Her mom was often aloof, preoccupied, and needy, unable to control her emotions. She didn't seek to comfort Emily, but sought out Emily to comfort her. From Emily's perspective, her mom was not someone who could protect and care for her, but rather someone who needed Emily to take care of her.

As illustrated in Emily's story, the messages of shame can be personalized not only through direct verbal communication, but through subtler indirect communication. More than the direct verbal exchanges she had with them, Emily's observation of her parents shaped her perception of them. Imagine what messages Emily received about herself from her parents. Imagine how many more positive interactions would be needed to counter the effects of these negative interactions. Having experienced feeling overlooked in times of need, Emily's shame was personalized: it told her she was not important, she didn't matter, and she was not worthy of being cared for.

## PERPETUATING SHAME
## THROUGH RELATIONSHIPS

Our internalized shame exacerbates our longing for connection in which we are fully accepted and loved for who we are. However, when we lost our connection with God, an inevitable relational disconnect in our human relationships followed as well. Genesis 3:7 says, "Then the eyes of both of them were opened, and they realized they were naked; so they sewed fig leaves together and made coverings for themselves." As this shift of "eyes being opened" occurred, immediately their innocent nakedness evolved to shameful nakedness. Their vulnerability was no longer an indication of closeness, but of shame, which set off a response to protect themselves by moving away from and turning against each other.

It was the longing for connection that brought Emily's parents together in the first place, but rather than easing the longing, each triggered the shame within the other, establishing a pattern of relating to one another that was reactive and self-protective. Emily's dad longed for connection but felt smothered by his wife's constant need for assurance to soothe her anxiety. So he kept her at a distance. Her mom longed for security, but her husband's emotional distance heightened her anxiety, causing her to react in emotional outbursts, which then erupted into conflicts in their marriage.

Our shame is perpetuated as the patterns we learn in our early relationships are repeated in every new relationship formed. One of the key patterns I have in my own relationships is my tendency to become a caregiver. Growing up as the oldest child of an immigrant family, I had the responsibility of making sure my younger siblings woke up and were fed before heading off to school. After school I was the one to make sure they did their homework before dinnertime.

In ministry I had the responsibility of caring for various groups in church over the years. I learned early on that my role as a caregiver was a key element in defining my identity, and I found my value in caring for other people. Obviously, this pattern also led me on the path of becoming a counselor, and it is still difficult for me not to care too much and to ask and receive care from others. To be clear, I do not think that caring for other people is a bad thing. The problem is that I've lived this way for the majority of my life in order to feel okay about myself and suppress the shame that something is wrong with me.

Relationship patterns begin forming very early in life. In fact, most experts agree that these patterns are set in the first year of our lives. Another term for relational connection is *attachment*, which is now a commonly known concept among many psychologists and laypeople. Attachment theory was introduced by John Bowlby, a psychiatrist and researcher in the early 1970s, who studied the formation of emotional bonds between primary caregivers and infants. He suggested that people possess an internal system called an *attachment system* that seeks to maintain closeness between infants and their primary caregivers. When a baby is distressed, the attachment system is activated and the baby will cry to reestablish closeness with the caregiver. When the baby is not distressed, the awareness of the caregiver's availability provides a sense of security for the baby to confidently explore his or her environment. Later Bowlby's work on attachment was further advanced by Mary Ainsworth, who demonstrated that there are particular patterns of attachment with corresponding behaviors and attitudes. From her observations, later confirmed by other researchers, four distinct attachment patterns were identified.[2]

## SECURE ATTACHMENTS

When children feel protected and sense that they have someone to rely on, they form *secure attachments*. This is the healthiest form of attachment, and children are comforted by the presence of their caregivers. Parents of securely attached children are emotionally attuned, meaning they are truly present and in tune with what their children may be feeling. These parents are also perceptive. They have a good sense of their children's needs, and most importantly, they are responsive when the child is in need. In turn, their children can better regulate their emotions, meaning they have the ability to exert control over their own emotional states and calm themselves. These children know when to seek emotional support and can handle being alone or with others. They can also connect with others with ease and are better at self-reflection.

This description of secure attachment gives us a clearer picture of how God relates to us when the Bible refers to him as our Abba Father who knows us intimately and who will never leave us or forsake us (Rom. 8:15; Deut. 31:8);

a Shepherd who lays down his life for us (John 10:11), and a fellow sufferer who identifies with our suffering and empathizes with us (Heb. 4:14–16). However, since the fall, it has become more challenging for us to experience secure attachments with other people. And as a result, it is harder for us to imagine God relating to us in these ways.

## INSECURE ATTACHMENTS

Although secure attachments are the ideal, it is estimated that only about 50 percent of the population exhibit this pattern. The other half display the opposite, referred to as *insecure attachments*. In Emily's story, we see two distinct patterns of insecure attachment.

Emily's behaviors and attitudes resemble the pattern of an *avoidant attachment*. Even though her parents provided her basic essentials like food and shelter, they were consistently unavailable and unresponsive to her *emotional* needs. They lacked the knowledge of how to support Emily when she was afraid as a child and could not empathize with her. In fact, she was yelled at to stop crying, which surely discouraged her from expressing her emotion. To maintain peace, Emily disregarded her own struggles and needs. As she got older, she had difficulty forming close relationships and even avoided making friends, fearing that being in a relationship would cause her harm, or, like her mom, her friends would need too much from her. Emily has trouble opening up to others. She is not very aware of her emotions and tends to ignore them. As noted before, she has trouble asking for help or for emotional support from others and is highly sensitive to disapproval or criticism. Because relationship patterns repeat themselves, it is likely that Emily learned some of these behaviors and attitudes from her dad, who also displays traits of avoidant attachment, minimizing emotions, pursuing accomplishments, and keeping people at a distance.

Emily's mom, however, shows patterns that resemble *ambivalent or anxious attachment*. Remember that Emily's mom grew up in an unstable home with lots of emotional distress. It's likely that her mother's parents were too consumed with their own emotional distress, making them inconsistent, unavailable, and often negligent. Likewise, Emily's mom was often unable to read what Emily needed because she was too preoccupied with her own emotional distress. Consequently, Emily's mom internalized the belief that other people are emotionally unreliable and the world is an unsafe place. As an adult, she was highly sensitive to rejection and abandonment in her relationship with her husband. As her marriage became increasingly unstable, she relied more and more on Emily to provide constant assurance and support to ease her anxiety.

The fourth and final attachment pattern is called *disorganized attachment*. This is an insecure attachment that develops when children are raised in an environment that elicits intense fear, often involving childhood trauma, neglect, and abuse. This painful pattern leads to difficulty trusting others, creating healthy relationships, and controlling emotions.

In Emily's story, neither her mom nor her dad were perceptive or attuned to Emily's emotional/relational needs. Her dad provided for her basic needs but discouraged emotional expression. Likewise, because her mom was consumed by her own emotions, Emily could not rely on her. As a result, Emily learned that other people are unavailable and cannot be trusted to care for her. Being exposed to the many conflicts between her parents and being insecurely attached to them, she felt that the world around her was unsafe and unpredictable. We can now see how Emily's attachment to her parents shaped her sense of self and others, as well as how she began to make sense of her world.

While we understand the effects of early relationship patterns on our development, it should also be noted that most parents who raise children with insecure attachments do love their children; they simply are not aware of their own relational patterns and how they are passed on from generation to generation. When we explore our past, it is not necessarily to assign blame or condemn our parents, though it is important to see what they did well and what they did wrong. We explore our past to better understand ourselves—the wounds that personalized our shame, what attitudes and beliefs we have adopted, and how we have learned to behave and live life as a result. Once we recognize our brokenness, we can move toward healing.

Patterns learned in relationships are repeated because we tend to do what is familiar to us even when we know it's dysfunctional and not good for us. The beliefs about ourselves and others, as well as our behavioral patterns in response, get wired into our brains and become automatic. Given some background on Emily's parents, we can better understand why they related to Emily as they did. Emily's dad repeatedly experienced feeling rejected, internalizing the message that he was not good enough. Emily's mom repeatedly experienced feeling unwanted, internalizing the message that she was a mistake and unlovable. However, neither of Emily's parents were aware of how their shame affected not only how they made sense of their own lives but how they related to one another and to their daughter. Because we are born with the innate sense of shame, our early relationships with our parents or caregivers become the first context for personalizing our shame, and then as we repeat the patterns, shame is perpetuated in one relationship after another.

Our identity includes multiple aspects of who we are, including the roles we play in our families, the roles we play in relationships or at work, our ethnic background, our gender and sexual orientation, and more. However, our primary identity is as people distinctly made in God's image, to be his treasured possession, his children to reflect and represent who he is. This truth about us should be the groundwork in which all aspects of our identity are rooted and lived out. Who God says we are gives us unchanging value and worth. However, as illustrated in Emily's story, we come into the world disconnected from the source from which to derive our identity, and as a result, though we are not aware of it, we live with the constant undercurrent of shame that colors how we make sense of ourselves and the world we live in.

Understanding Emily's family background, we have a better sense of why she may be feeling hopeless and ashamed in the present, but there is more to her story. When sin entered the world, it didn't just affect individual hearts. Sin invaded and infected all of creation, inflicting wounds and making pain and suffering inevitable for all of us. We'll learn more about that in the next chapter.

## *Reflection*

Consider your relationship with your parents as a child. Early caregivers are the first to influence how we see ourselves and others. Reflect on the following questions:

1. Using adjectives, how would you describe your parents or other significant caregivers in your life?
2. As a child, did you feel important or special to them? Did you feel you could approach your caregivers for comfort and help?
3. What messages did your caregivers convey about you as you were growing up?
4. Do these messages about you readily come to mind in the present?

# THREE

# WOUNDS THAT SHAPE
# WHO WE ARE

**M**ost of us can recall a painful event or an experience that affected us in significant ways and changed how we felt about ourselves, other people, and the world around us. Listening to devastating stories of pain and suffering is a huge part of what I do. Over the years, I've learned that *how* people make sense of their experiences is even more important than *what* they've actually experienced, and that what people experience in the present moment is never void of influences from their past.

As I've shared, one of the most pronounced wounds that personalized and reinforced my own internalized shame came from my experiences growing up as a child of Korean immigrants in America. Before coming to America, I liked going to school, but school became a dreadful thing after arriving here. For the first two years, as a third and a fourth grader, I sat at the back of the class with paper and a box of crayons, separated from the rest of the kids. I spent most of the hours at school preoccupied with trying to figure out how to avoid the bullies and safely get home. I was physically assaulted by peers and emotionally scarred by teachers, who seemed negligent and treated me differently from the other students.

In these experiences, I repeatedly felt humiliated and discarded, deeply embedding the message that I was defective and never good enough, an outsider who did not belong. This contributes to my own problem of *shame*, as I discussed in chapter 2. Shame is the innate and ever-present sense that we are not enough, which is initially reinforced and personalized in our primary relationships. Shame is often invisible to us and unaddressed. However, *core hurts* result from the experiences we may remember all too well. They reinforce our shame and trigger our greatest fears and insecurities. How we react to them is often not helpful and at times is even harmful to ourselves or others.

The fall introduced evil into God's creation and affected everything, and the whole created order no longer reflects what God intended. Since the fall, we experience life in this world as both sufferers and sinners. In Romans 8:22 we read that all of creation has been groaning as in the pain of childbirth and that we are groaning as we wait eagerly for our adoption and the redemption of our bodies. So every relationship, family, community, or social system— including every church and even our own bodies—is affected by sin. Moreover, natural calamities and diseases, which are often unrelated to personal sin, inflict us. We are not only born with an innate sense of shame from being separated from our Creator, but we also live life in a fallen world in which we experience all kinds of hardship. Pain and suffering are part of our stories that shape who we are.

Each of our life stories contains wounds or core hurts stemming from dysfunctional family relationships and individual losses, as well as personal traumas like abuse or illness. Core hurts are a result of repeated emotion-laden experiences that are painful, that personalize and reinforce our internalized shame. For example, when Emily's father yelled at her to stop crying, she might have initially felt scared, which was appropriate. But as she was told, "Stop crying!" over and over again, and no one addressed her fear, she began to feel unseen and devalued. These repeated experiences of feeling unseen became a core hurt that conveyed the message that she doesn't matter, that she is insignificant. So core hurts are more than feelings; they are an accumulation of painful wounds that convey shame messages about us that perpetuate more wounding. These core hurts personalize our shame and form an unconscious appraisal system or a template that makes sense of what happens to us. And this template skews our perceptions and interpretations, hurting us even more. So, to understand how to help Emily in the present, we have to know what actually happened to her in the past.

In this chapter, we will further explore how our wounds set us up for more wounding as our past continues to invade our present experiences. We will also explore how core hurts could impact our bodies as image bearers who exist in physical bodies.

## OUR PAST AFFECTING OUR PRESENT

The core hurts from our parental relationships shape the initial template for making sense of ourselves and others. Our early caregivers are the first source from which we derive our identity. Repetitions of relational experiences that share a common emotional core, like Emily's experiences with her parents, are encoded in our brains and work like templates.[1] These are unconscious mental representations that work much like our implicit biases. These templates, formed from experiences in early relationships with caregivers, shape our relational interpretations and subsequent patterns of relationship that become the foundation of our knowledge of self and others. These templates provide the blueprint for how to perceive and interact with others, including what to expect in social interactions, which leads to how we see our world. This means that what we experienced in our past, particularly in our significant relationships, has the potential to affect our present in substantial ways.

Here's how this happens. With advancements in neuroscience, we know much better now how the brain works—how it makes us rational, irrational, reflective, and reactive at different times. For example, many of us have heard of the right brain and left brain distinction. The left brain is responsible for processing verbal information to help us think logically and organize our thoughts, while the right brain is responsible for processing emotional, nonverbal information, such as facial expressions, tone of voice, eye contact, gestures, and body language. It is estimated that 60 to 90 percent of communication is nonverbal.

Our brain processes nonverbal information much faster than verbal information, and the nonverbals are more enduring in our memory. This means that people will remember your tone of voice or facial expressions more readily than your spoken words. This might be a little bit alarming for parents, but we know now that the right brain develops first! As infants, we cannot process verbal information until we're about eighteen to twenty-four months old. So the nonverbal information shapes our beliefs about ourselves and others from the very beginning, and it gets stored in our *implicit memory.* Implicit means that it is not in our conscious awareness. These beliefs, then, work like reflexes and automatically serve as templates to make interpretations about the self and others in every interaction.

For Emily, her unconscious beliefs about herself as insignificant and worthless correspond with her view of others as unreliable, cold, and harsh. It is likely that she sees her former boyfriend and her former boss as unreliable, cold, and harsh in her present situation. She was fired from her job, her sense of security, in spite of all of her efforts to meet her boss's expectations. Her former boyfriend ended the relationship at a time of great distress for Emily, two weeks after she was fired. In her present situation, she is not only feeling the pain of her present circumstances, but her present suffering is being added to the accumulation of pain from her past. Knowing this about Emily, we can make sense of her feelings of hopelessness and her inability to get out of bed. Her emotional and behavioral reactions to the present are exacerbated by her past.

Early caregiver relationships are critical in forming our relational templates, but these early templates can be changed over time as we live through significant life-altering experiences. For me, the dynamics in my relationship with my parents shifted notably when we immigrated to America. I am sure many immigrants can relate, but my parents had to work very hard just to make sure we had a place to live and food to eat. They worked opposite schedules from one another so that one of them could always be home with us. As I remember it, most of their hours at home were spent coaching me to care for my siblings and catching up on their sleep. As an adult looking back at my parents' lives, I find it quite remarkable how they oriented themselves to a new country where everything was unfamiliar. However, as a child, I knew they were not only unavailable but also incapable of helping me. My parents did not have to tell me how hard it was to "survive" here. I heard their distress in the sound of their voices. I saw on their faces how weary they were, lacking sleep from working long hours and caring for us, their young children. Even as an eight-year-old, I did not want to burden them any more than they already were, and they did not have the capacity to inquire about and listen to how I was doing. Even though they were very affirming of me and my good behavior, I often felt alone in dealing with the troubles I had to face outside of our home. What I was going through was not a priority, and therefore I was not important. My experiences of feeling incompetent, sitting in the back of the classroom, feeling discarded by the teachers who seemed uncaring and biased, and feeling humiliated by the emotional and physical bullying from my peers had greater impact on my sense of self, in part because I perceived that my parents were not available and were incapable of helping me.

How does my past affect my present life? Despite knowing my history and its influence on me, my usual pattern is to try to deal with my distresses alone. Growing up, I had learned to minimize and suppress the emotional weight of my experiences to deal with them on my own. Now, when my core hurts are triggered, I know something is off, but I have trouble labeling and expressing what is going on within me. And rather than asking for help, I tend to withdraw to struggle on my own. Having said this, I want to make clear that I am not doomed to this pattern. I do not see every person as unavailable and incapable of caring for me. In my lifetime, I've had many experiences of feeling cared for and others being available to me. However, when things happen that trigger my core hurts and I am overwhelmed with feeling incompetent, discarded, and humiliated, it is hard for me to avoid the interpretations that reinforce my relational templates: that I am not important, not good enough, and defective while others are unavailable, incapable, and indifferent. Our templates become a default lens of making sense of ourselves and others, even in our present experiences.

## OUR CORE HURTS
## AFFECT OUR BODIES

Relational wounds in significant relationships are one category of core hurts that we experience. As I've described, they form relational templates that subsequently affect our present relationships and how we make sense of as well as respond to our world. However, because sin affected all of creation, our core hurts also stem from our losses and personal traumas, which affect our *physical bodies*. People who struggle with emotional issues like anxiety or panic attacks are unlikely to struggle only in their minds. They also struggle with symptoms in their bodies—in the way they breathe and sit, in how their shoulders slump and cave inward, in their sleep patterns, and in their digestive processes.

Most of us are familiar with the classic symptoms of post-traumatic stress disorder (PTSD), such as flashbacks or nightmares, that clearly demonstrate the connection between the effects of traumatic experiences and our ability to sleep or function. But living in a broken world, all of us are affected by experiences of trauma, whether we realize it or not. Things happen that are beyond our control, like the COVID-19 pandemic or the prolonged trauma of profound neglect or poverty. However, even more than the experience of trauma itself, how we *deal* with our traumatic experiences matters more in how that trauma will affect us both psychologically and physically. When we don't acknowledge our painful experiences and process the trauma they've caused, our symptoms of trauma can worsen over time.

Gina came to see me because she had recently experienced several panic attacks. As she shared more, it seemed that the timing of when the panic attacks began correlated with a marriage proposal from her fiancé. She shared that it was a beautiful moment, one that she will always remember, and expressed how deeply in love she was with her fiancé. Yet at the same time, she felt a strange sense of disconnect. She felt her heart rate increase and her body stiffen a bit, but she wasn't sure if she was genuinely moved or afraid in that moment. She fought the urge to run away, and the evening ended just fine. Since that day, though, she has been distressed, had problems focusing at work and sleeping at night, and has been having nightmares. She has also been contemplating whether she should end the relationship.

As we explored more of her story, her trauma became more apparent. She had an estranged relationship with her father, who was cut off from the family since she was a child. Although she did not have any explicit memory of sexual abuse by her father, she remembered feeling uneasy and at times disgusted in his presence. As she became more curious about her past, she eventually learned that her parents divorced shortly after her mom discovered there was abuse. Even though Gina did not recall the abuse and had not suffered a prolonged period of abuse, her body remembered. In the moment in which she felt most connected with her fiancé, in that romantic instance of emotional and sexual arousal, her body remembered the similar sensations she experienced as a child being abused by her father. As illustrated in Gina's story, our past can intrude in our present because our bodies are also affected by our experiences of pain and suffering.

Growing up in the church, I've noticed that the predominant emphasis has often been on nurturing the soul, but not as much on valuing our bodies. In fact, at times I've gotten the sense that our bodies are irrelevant to our spiritual maturity or that our bodies are less than sacred, a part of ourselves that we need to bear with or transcend and overcome. The Bible, however, presents a very different view of our physical bodies. Looking back to creation in Genesis 2:7, "The LORD God formed a man from the dust of the ground and breathed into his nostrils the breath of life, and the man became a living being." Our physical body is God's intentional creative act. Moreover, we know that Jesus came to us in human form as a baby (Luke 2:12). He was born as an infant and developed into adulthood. He experienced life as one of us with human senses. When Jesus came to us in human likeness (Phil. 2:6–7), his incarnation itself demonstrated the greatest complement to our physical bodies. And our bodies are fearfully and wonderfully made (Ps. 139:13–14), operating in wondrous ways to keep us alive. Parts of our bodies work together to keep us breathing, our organs functioning, and coordinating responses and reflexes. Our bodies work in ways to help us adapt to our environment. We are spiritual beings designed to live and have physical experiences relating to one another and to all of creation in our bodies. Our bodies should not be negated or considered less important than our souls, nor should the body be equated with the "flesh," which is often synonymous with our sinful nature.

What we have discovered through science bears out what we see in Scripture: the body and soul are linked in intricate ways. Prolonged stress and emotional trauma affect our bodies as well as our souls. In recent years, studies have enlightened us about the intricate connection between our inherited DNA and the environmental factors that affect our development. A foundational study by the CDC and Kaiser Permanente in the mid-1990s found that exposure to traumatic events or circumstances in the first seventeen years of life can dramatically affect a person's brain development, immune system, hormones, and even the way our DNA is read and transcribed. Those who are exposed to prolonged traumatic experiences as children have triple the lifetime risk of heart disease and lung cancer, and a twenty-year difference in life expectancy.[2]

Since we are given a physical body so that we can exist and experience life here on earth, it makes sense that our bodies would also be affected by what happened to us, particularly our core hurts. Through subsequent studies on childhood trauma, we now know that developmental stressors can make a huge difference in the way our bodies and brains function. Some stress is needed for our development—for example, the stress of going to school for the first time, or the stress we experience when we have to take a test or interview for a job. However, extreme, prolonged, chaotic patterns of stress that activate our stress response systems in a persistent way weigh tremendously on our physical bodies, including our hearts and other organs. This then causes our brain and parts of our central nervous system to malfunction or function less optimally. In fact, neuroscientists now say that these chaotic, persistent experiences can actually change the biology of the brain.[3] As a result, we can develop not only cognitive or learning problems but also emotional problems like anxiety, depression, and the inability to regulate or balance our emotions.

Dr. Bruce Perry, a psychiatrist and researcher, explains how we, and particularly our bodies, are affected by traumatic experiences.[4] Our bodies pick up sensory input from the environment through our senses, and then our brains organize this information and use it to participate in everyday activities. Our stress regulatory networks in the lower parts of the brain receive information from the outside world through the senses—sight, sound, smell, taste, and touch—and create templates and associations, which get stored in our implicit memory to make sense of what we are experiencing very quickly. And based on our interpretations, we know how to respond to what's happening.

Our stress regulatory networks have what we call a baseline level of activation. Normally, when our stress is activated, it peaks, but it eventually comes back down to the baseline as our stress subsides. However, when we experience patterns of adversity over time, such as abuse, neglect, racial trauma, or poverty, our stress response system will be thrown off. Apparently these repeated experiences of distress do not allow the stress response system to return to the baseline. So, even when we are minimally stimulated, the body signals the brain to stay activated, which then ends up changing the baseline. In other words, what we experience in our environment primes our stress response systems for more continued stress. Our childhood experiences influence how we make sense of life and also alter the physiology of our brain as the baseline for activation shifts. As a result, in a person who has experienced multiple or persistent traumatic events, the stress response system gets sensitized and even an ordinary stressor may feel like a major crisis.[5]

For Emily, the sensitization to specific stressors began early in her life. She was exposed to the raised voices of her parents yelling at each other, the sound of objects breaking, the door slamming, an angry dad and a sobbing mom. As an infant, she didn't have the tools to understand what was happening around her, but her stress response system was activated on a regular basis. Her reaction of being afraid was not only an emotional response, but it involved her body. Imagine a frightened infant crying. Unable to make sense of what was really happening around her, young Emily probably felt frantic. As her heart rate increased, she probably became flushed and her little body tightened as she shrieked and cried. The exposure to her parents' conflicts led to Emily's sensitization to abrupt, loud noises and disorderly environments. At home, even a sigh from her dad made her heart race as she feared that another conflict might erupt. All of this made Emily hypervigilant to chaos, certain noises, interpersonal conflicts, and emotional experiences like feeling afraid and out of control.

We can imagine that even Emily's move to New York City, with its noise and fast pace, could have heightened her stress. She had counted on her job to be the more predictable, controllable aspect of her huge transition to the city. However, within weeks, what she counted on had become an unsafe place. Her stress response system went on alert whenever she noticed her boss's facial expressions or tone of voice. Sensitized to these cues, whenever her boss expressed his dissatisfaction, either spoken or unspoken, the activation would peak, causing Emily to feel highly anxious, which would often lead to physical symptoms like indigestion, muscle tension, and insomnia. Even when she was not working, for example, when she was out with her boyfriend, Emily's stress response system would not let her relax and recoup. Imagine the strain on her body for the stretch of eight months in her new job.

Even though many of us can acknowledge what happened to us, often we are not fully aware of the impact of what we experienced. Many years may have passed and we may have even talked about our wounds, yet we can still be stuck in our past, living in response to our past experiences in our present reality. In the next chapter, as we continue exploring what is the *real* problem, we'll examine how we try to manage and soothe our pain and suffering.

# *Reflection*

We all experience hardships in life. Consider your life story and select a significant event that affected you. Write your responses to the following:

1. Describe the significant event.
2. How did you feel about yourself at the time of this event (rejected, betrayed, neglected, etc.)?
3. Have you felt these same feelings at other times in your life?
4. Do you experience these feelings in the present?
5. What message do these feelings communicate about you (I am inadequate, I am hopeless, etc.)?

FOUR

# WAYS WE PROTECT
# OURSELVES AND
# ASSERT AN IDENTITY

Nobody likes to be in pain, and so we are motivated to fix it. But oddly enough, we don't treat every pain the same way. When we get a toothache or break a bone, most of us will seek medical treatment to alleviate the physical pain and fix what caused it. Yet when we experience emotional pain, rather than giving it our attention, many people will avoid dealing with it or even suppress it. Perhaps we don't think it is *real* pain. Yet there is now scientific evidence that legitimizes our emotional pain as authentic pain. Research shows that when people feel emotional pain, it activates the same areas of the brain as when we feel physical pain.[1]

So our emotional pain—the pain of our shame and core

hurts—is real. We feel it. Being separated from God and the subsequent experience of internalized shame is painful. The sense that something is wrong with us makes us desperately long for somebody to tell us we are okay, that we are acceptable. And to alleviate that pain, we construct a solution of our own to deal with it.

Just like Adam and Eve, we are motivated to hide our shame even more actively as our shame is personalized and reinforced in our own life experiences, forming our core hurts. Our shame—plus the core hurts that aggravate our shame—is painful and we don't like it, so in the context of our pain, we develop ways to deal with it to survive our suffering. The more I listen to people's stories, the more I am astonished by their resilience and the innovative ways they adapt to agonizing pain. I believe our ability to adapt for survival is a wonderful trait, an image-bearing quality. Yet every good thing has the potential to become harmful in the hearts of fallen beings.

Recently I've been thinking about my younger self and how I sought to acculturate and adapt to a foreign country. I didn't speak the language. I didn't feel like I had anyone to help me, especially when I was being taunted and bullied. But as an eight-year-old child, something inside me said, *I'm not going to let them win.* Even though I felt scared and hurt, even when I was physically pinned against a wall and my box of forty-eight crayons was taken away, I acted as if the name-calling and shoving in the hallways didn't affect me. I showed up at school day after day.

What allowed me to face my fears, numb the hurts, and show up at school every day for two years? I developed a strategy to appear tough by suppressing my pain, and this strategy helped me survive through those years. So there is a sense in which our ability to develop a strategy to survive and adapt in the midst of adversity should be celebrated. It got me through a time in my life when I had nowhere else to go, no one to turn to. Yet at the same time, there is always a price to pay, and we should be aware of the damage that results if we don't pay attention to our pain. I developed a strategy to project an image of courage and strength and to hide parts of me—my fears and my hurts—that I considered vulnerabilities. This kept me safe from my attackers. Yet this same strategy also kept me from getting the help I needed and ultimately prevented me from really being known and feeling accepted by others throughout my lifetime.

People who experience the same events and circumstances can respond in very different ways. Just as we develop relational patterns with other people, we also develop unique patterns that correlate to our stories to help us manage and survive the really hard stuff we face. In fact, we develop multiple strategies over time and learn which strategy is most effective in a specific circumstance. These strategies are a key component of our stories, and they provide us with insight about who we are. They deeply affect our identity formation. Again, I want to stress that our ability to adapt to what is happening around us by utilizing these strategies is not bad in and of itself. Often it is our only option to survive. But when we rely on our strategies to do something that they are not designed to do—address our shame and give us an identity—they become idolatrous.

Much of my understanding about idols has been

influenced by the teaching of Tim Keller as I have sat under his ministry for many years. In particular, his book *Counterfeit Gods* teaches us that good things can evolve and become ultimate things, things we base our identity on.[2] So while our survival strategies are good ways to help us adapt to living in a broken world, those same strategies can also evolve and become idolatrous, often manifesting in two ways: we hide what we think is bad or shameful, and we assert what is good and worthy about ourselves. We engage in both of these patterns, and both patterns are our self-reliant ways to fix the effects of sin—our shame and core hurts. We see this in Genesis 3:7 in how Adam and Eve sewed fig leaves together, a temporary strategy to cover up their shame. In a similar way, our idolatrous strategies suppress the pain of the core hurts that trigger our shame and justify and invalidate our shame so we feel okay about ourselves.

In this chapter, we will look at how these strategies develop, their complexity, and their connection to our identity. Then we'll explore the ineffectiveness of our idolatrous strategies and how these same failed strategies can become part of what is wrong with us, our system of self-redemption.

## THE STORY BEHIND OUR STRATEGIES

Our strategies develop in the context of our pain, and much like our shame and core hurts, these strategies operate unconsciously and automatically to preemptively manage our pain and suffering. However, when our strategies evolve and become the basis of our identity, they are idolatrous.

Consider Emily's story. Throughout her early years, her core hurts of feeling unseen and devalued were repeatedly triggered, confirming again and again that she was insignificant, unlovable, and worthless. Subsequently, she believed that other people in the world are unreliable, cold, and harsh. Emily believed she was on her own, navigating through the dangerous terrain of life. In this place of pain, Emily's strategy began to form to help her cope with and survive her pain.

By the time she was a young child, Emily was hypervigilant about complying with her dad's demands to keep him from his angry outbursts. She tolerated the conflicts between her parents without crying, tried to care for herself and clean up her messes as instructed, and sought to manage her feelings of fear on her own. When she entered school, her teachers noticed that she was smart, and Emily was rewarded for her academic excellence. We can imagine how this new experience of being seen and approved must have been a relief and a delight to Emily. In fifth grade, Emily was noticed for her musical talents. Soon even more people were noticing her and paying her compliments. Emily had figured out a way to be seen and to feel significant. Since that time, she has intentionally used her musical talents and academic success as a way of being seen and admired. Over time her strategies became less about surviving her pain and more about suppressing her core hurts and asserting a significant and worthy identity. Her strategies evolved, and they became a way for her to feel all right about herself. Even though she attended church and considered herself a practicing

Christian, Jesus' salvation was not something that she realized could heal her of her past or change the way she saw herself and others. In fact, her attendance and involvement at church also became part of her strategy. Being perceived as a good Christian, doing the right things, and serving the church also became idolatrous, a God replacement that she relied on to redeem herself.

## THE COMPLEXITY OF IDOLATRY AND ITS CONNECTION TO IDENTITY

What is idolatry? Idolatry can be simply understood as any object, person, or pursuit that becomes more important than God in our lives. It begins with something good—academic achievement, romantic love, a goal to pursue—and progresses until that good becomes something ultimate for us. Like anything else, the strategies we develop as a way to cope with and survive the pain of our stories can become idolatrous as we depend on them to redeem our shame-based identity. Though our idolatrous strategies are proactive ways in which we try to suppress our pain and feel okay about ourselves, the mechanism behind these strategies is complex. What turns these good things into ultimate things involves the motivations or the desires that rule our hearts, what we might call our *deep idols*.[3]

Deep idols are the innate desires within us, desires that have become disordered by sin. The chief innate desires are the desires for power, control, approval, and comfort. Again, these are good desires, reflections of our image bearing, but they have evolved into inordinate desires or demands. They operate in the subconscious realm, beneath our awareness.

Closely related to these deep idols are our *surface idols*—any tangible objects, persons, or pursuits that become idols, such as money, career, sex, or children. Our deep idols are the *underlying* motivation that fuels our pursuit of good things, evolving them into ultimate things (surface idols). Surface idols are much more recognizable, and we are more willing to admit we have them. For example, an executive who works too much may admit he is a workaholic. However, what we often fail to recognize is that beneath the surface idol we have deeper, unconscious desires that have become excessive. These deeper desires have been misplaced onto created things, evolving these objects, persons, and pursuits into ultimate things. These deep idols combined with our surface idols make up our idolatrous strategies.

We switch surface idols quite easily depending on our circumstances and life stages, but our deep idols are more enduring and persistent throughout our lives. An individual may let go of his idol of work but replace it with an idol of religion, leaving his underlying deep idol of *approval* intact and unchallenged. On the outside, it may appear that he has changed considerably, but he is still driven by a need to be affirmed by others for his identity. When we recognize that something in our lives—such as a career, family, money, success, fitness, beauty, fame, relationship, or leisure—has become too important to us, we also must consider the desire in our hearts that drives us to make these created things into idols.

Our hearts have four basic desires: power, control, approval, and comfort. These four desires can also be categorized into two distinct patterns of idolatry: mastery and avoidance. The deep idols of power and control correlate with

## THE FOUR DEEP IDOLS

| Mastery | Definition / over-desire | Fears / greatest nightmare |
|---------|--------------------------|----------------------------|
| **Power** | Over-desire for significance through success, winning, and influence. May feel the need to be right, the best, competent, outstanding, "special" person. In fact, you may hear your clients assert how "good" they are. | Fears humiliation and meaninglessness. Wants to avoid feeling insignificant. |
| **Control** | Over-desire for certainty, which exhibits through control of self, environment, others—not necessarily by dominance, but more by control over doing something—working hard, being self-disciplined, upholding standards. They may seek certainty and may seek to be self-sufficient. | Fears uncertainty, criticism, and may want to avoid feelings of uselessness, irrelevance (*I don't matter*), which may lead to a sense of being invisible (non-existent). |

the mastery pattern, which is motivated by a desire to assert our goodness, while approval and comfort correlate with the avoidance pattern, which is motivated to hide what we consider bad about us. Each of us has all four of these innate

| Impact on relationship dynamics | Problem emotions |
|---|---|
| Others are either idealized (corresponds to desire) or devalued (corresponds to fear). Others feel used by them. | Dominant emotion is anger expressed outwardly. |
| Affirmation/praise from others is not a priority, or they do not depend on it, because they are their own judge and they know that they are right and good. | |
| Others feel condemned around them. They believe others rely on them. Others are drawn to their capacity to perform (very capable) and solve problems, but others are kept at a distance. They usually do not feel much affect toward others. | Dominant emotion is feeling worried or anxious. |
| Social distance is present, while power people seek a wider social circle. | |

*continued*

| *Avoidance* | Definition / over-desire | Fears / greatest nightmare |
|---|---|---|
| **Approval** | Over-desire to please, to get affirmation and acceptance through relationships by helping and meeting others' needs/desires.<br><br>They need to get positive feedback, to provide services so that others need them. They may be susceptible to codependency. | Fears rejection, avoids conflicts, and may struggle with cowardice. |
| **Comfort** | Over-desire for avoidance of pain/ stress by seeking freedom from responsibilities, expectations, and anything that may feel unpleasant by seeking immediate gratification through addictive behaviors or through numbing and escaping. | Fears stress and demands and may seek privacy. |

desires, as well as a tendency toward one deep idol within each pattern, but we develop a dominant deep idol based on our inherent makeup and the environment we were raised in. This dominant deep idol gets mobilized more frequently, especially when our shame and core hurts are triggered.

Our preference for a deep idol develops early in our childhood and endures throughout our lives. Growing up with

| Impact on relationship dynamics | Problem emotions |
|---|---|
| Others are feared or idealized. Others may feel smothered because client needs their affirmation for the client to feel worthy.<br><br>Others tend to see them as warm, friendly, considerate, nonaggressive.<br><br>Absorbs criticism and may easily say that they are bad or wrong. | Dominant emotional reaction is implosion of fear. Avoids situations for fear of conflict and avoids people for fear of rejection.<br><br>Usually seeks connections with others to soothe their fear. |
| Others may feel neglected or annoyed because they may seem indifferent and may be unproductive. They do not believe that others care about them, thus the lack of response to others. They tend to be passive aggressive. | Dominant emotions experienced are restlessness, boredom, and weariness as a result of detaching, consequently feeling meaninglessness and isolation. |

unreliable parents, Emily's greatest fear is uncertainty, and so it makes sense that she desired to secure a safe and stable environment, sought to control her own body and emotions to tolerate the chaos at home, and attempted to control her parents' emotions to survive her childhood. The deep idol of *control* motivated her toward behavioral patterns in which she burdened herself to do everything—perform well, keep busy by doing, care for others, and never ask for help. Given her tendency to feel overly responsible, she blamed herself and was likely highly critical of herself when things did not turn out the way she wanted them to.

Contrarily, if Emily had been motivated by *power*, we would have seen her align with her mom as the idealized parent, clinging to her and becoming part of the emotional chaos of the conflicts through her own emotional outbursts. She most likely would not have complied with her dad's demands, but rather would have tried to dominate his anger with her own emotional outbursts. When people are motivated by the deep idol of power, we notice a pattern of demanding, condescending, or critical behavior toward others as a way to dominate them. The deep idol of power motivates us to assert *I am good* by putting others down because we greatly fear humiliation and feeling insignificant. Those with the deep idol of control keep people at a distance, while those with the deep idol of power tend to have a wider social circle but often see others as competitors and do not feel a responsibility to care for them.

When *approval* becomes an inordinate desire, people are agreeable with others to the point of overpromising and underdelivering. While those with a deep idol of control may avoid conflicts to focus on doing, folks with a deep idol of approval will avoid conflicts for fear of rejection. Approval folks also tend to have a wide social circle, but they seek this as a way to secure a sense of connection and to get others' affirmation. If Emily was inclined toward the deep idol of approval, she might have behaved similarly, going to her mom after a fight, not to console her, but rather to be consoled by her mom. She would have craved her dad's acknowledgment of her gifts, his pats on her head and back, rather than being suspicious of his affirmations. We would have seen Emily's social circle widen instead of staying small as her world expanded beyond her family. She would not have restricted her admirers but would have engaged with as many of them as possible.

If Emily was motivated by *comfort*, it is unlikely that she would have tried to console her mom. She would have shut down and stayed detached from her parents' conflicts and engaged in self-soothing/disassociating behaviors like rocking with her favorite blanket as a young child or reading a book as a youth. To those who prefer the comfort idol, avoiding pain and distress is their primary drive. They seek freedom from the responsibilities of life and the expectations of others, and are motivated to seek immediate gratification to alleviate whatever is unpleasant as much as possible. Later in life, as Emily's responsibilities expanded with her development, we might have seen her doing less and less or even distracting herself with some sort of addictive behavior to escape feeling stressed.

Again, our desires for power, control, approval, and comfort are not bad desires, but we should be aware that these desires can become disproportionate and drive us to make created things (objects, persons, or pursuits) into ultimate things. Since our deep idols are part of the idolatrous strategies we employ in relating to others and our environment, others can often observe them in us even though we ourselves are unaware of them. People, sometimes within the church, may even applaud us for certain behaviors when they can't see the brokenness that is driving them. The information we receive from others then reinforces the patterns that develop into our strategies.

For example, in my own story I was affirmed for being a good older sister and being responsible beyond my age. As a result, my pattern of overfunctioning in relationships continued in various caregiving roles in my personal life, in ministry, and in my professional life as a counselor. And I continue to receive affirmation about my capacity to care for other people, reinforcing this pattern. Caring well for others became one of my strategies of control to feel okay about myself. This is why when my supervisor pointed out what I perceived to be a rookie mistake as a counselor, my shame was provoked and I felt ashamed and incompetent.

## INEFFECTIVENESS OF OUR IDOLATROUS STRATEGIES

When our idolatrous strategies are working for us, they are effectively giving us an identity. We may even experience a sense of relief when our desires are met, at least for a time, but the relief we feel does not last very long. With each desire, there is a corresponding fear that will not allow us to rest. The fear in us keeps us perpetually striving to make sure that what we fear will not become reality. We will strive to assert what is "good" about us and hide what is "bad" about us. My desire to lessen the burdens of my parents resulted in my tendency to overburden myself in relationships, but my corresponding fear of feeling useless or irrelevant perpetuated a pattern of overfunctioning in almost all of my relationships.

Similarly, Emily was affirmed for performing well and projecting an image of having her life all together. So it was not an option for her to reach out to others, even when she lost her job and was heartbroken by the end of her relationship. In both of our stories, the longing in us to be known and accepted, to be counted worthy, perpetuated a cycle of striving for more.

But our strategies don't ultimately work, and it's not only because our desires and their corresponding fears create a vicious cycle of perpetual striving in us. We also live in a broken world with broken people, and we will face situations in which our idolatrous strategies will fail us. When our strategies fail, we will not only experience the pain associated with our present situation, but also the accumulation of pain from our past, which is called reactive emotions. These reactive emotions are what we experience when our desires are unmet, our core hurts are triggered, and our shame is provoked. These reactive emotions trigger the most conscious, outward set of reactions, often described as the fight, flight, or freeze response. These behavioral reactions occur in a split second without our realizing the subconscious components at play. In Emily's case, when she initially lost her job, she became hypervigilant about finding another one. However, when her strategy of working hard did not produce the result she needed to feel secure, she became depressed and got stuck (a "freeze" response), unable to even get out of bed.

We develop strategies to avoid pain, but the problem with our idolatrous strategies is that they do not save us from pain when they fail. And we adopt them to give us an identity, but they do not permanently set us free from the preoccupation of knowing who we are and where our value comes from. At best they help us to feel better about ourselves for a time. Internally the fear that corresponds with our desire keeps us striving for more power, control, approval, and comfort to extinguish our pain and secure an acceptable identity again and again. These idolatrous strategies keep us trapped in a cycle of continuous striving, especially as we encounter new situations in which our strategies don't work and can't "save" us. The strategies that were supposed to help us survive and protect us become things that entangle us and keep us stuck. Our failed strategies come with overwhelming feelings (reactive emotions) and impulsive behaviors (behavioral reactions), which are difficult to manage, add to our problems, and affect our sense of self and worth.

We are all born with the inclination to rely on ourselves, to develop strategies to deal with our pain and hide our shame. Even though these strategies are frequently ineffective, they are hard to relinquish. We cling to them and use them without thinking about them because we do not want to see or feel our pain.

## PUTTING ALL THE PROBLEMS TOGETHER

Most people seek counseling because of the pain of reactive emotions or behaviors or because of some troubling situation in their lives. To this point, we've seen that the underlying problem is much bigger than people are aware of. But to "fix" anything, we need to know what is broken. Although our physical and psychological brokenness is readily acknowledged in counseling, our spiritual brokenness is often overlooked—or at least not taken seriously enough. However, the broken state of our soul lies at the core of what is really wrong with us, and it is this that leads to thoughts, feelings, and behaviors that affect us and our relationships.

In chapter 1, I introduced the system of self-redemption (SOSR) as an attempt to comprehensively identify the problem we are facing, because when we make sense of the problem, we can help people experience God's healing and his power to change. The SOSR includes all aspects of human brokenness: our internalized shame, the core hurts that reinforce our shame, and our ineffective idolatrous strategies that elicit reactive emotions and responses that add to the problem we are dealing with.

We know from Emily's story that from the time she entered the world, she had a sense that there was something wrong with her—that she fell short of some standard of perfection. As she interacted with the world, and especially with her primary caregivers, her shame became personalized. Emily internalized a sense that she is insignificant and unlovable, having experienced feeling unseen and devalued as her parents were entangled by their own emotional mess in conflicts with each other.

As a result, Emily developed several strategies fueled by her desire for certainty and security. She sought to perform well in school, kept busy by serving at church, cared for others, and projected an image that she had it all together.

However, when she could not secure another job after being fired and her boyfriend ended their relationship, her core hurts of feeling unseen and devalued were triggered, and her shame—that she is insignificant and unlovable—was evoked. The gravity of this pain then led to her feeling hopeless and alone, causing her to shut down and remain stuck in bed.

## SYSTEM OF SELF-REDEMPTION
(What do I need to do to feel okay about myself?)

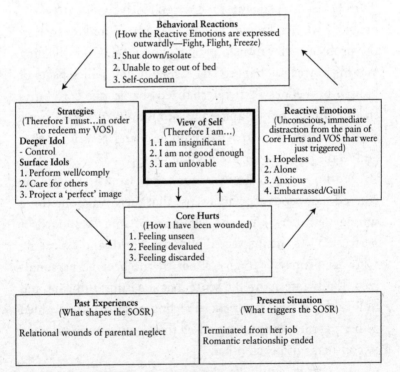

**Behavioral Reactions**
(How the Reactive Emotions are expressed outwardly—Fight, Flight, Freeze)
1. Shut down/isolate
2. Unable to get out of bed
3. Self-condemn

**Strategies**
(Therefore I must...in order to redeem my VOS)
**Deeper Idol**
- Control
**Surface Idols**
1. Perform well/comply
2. Care for others
3. Project a 'perfect' image

**View of Self**
(Therefore I am...)
1. I am insignificant
2. I am not good enough
3. I am unlovable

**Reactive Emotions**
(Unconscious, immediate distraction from the pain of Core Hurts and VOS that were just triggered)
1. Hopeless
2. Alone
3. Anxious
4. Embarrassed/Guilt

**Core Hurts**
(How I have been wounded)
1. Feeling unseen
2. Feeling devalued
3. Feeling discarded

**Past Experiences**
(What shapes the SOSR)

Relational wounds of parental neglect

**Present Situation**
(What triggers the SOSR)

Terminated from her job
Romantic relationship ended

Ironically, Emily's strategy to obtain an identity actually resulted in reexperiencing her core hurts and reinforcing the sense that she is indeed insignificant and unlovable. Even though it looks like Emily's problem is her present circumstances, we know the deeper problem is much more than that. The system of self-redemption is the real problem we need to address with her.

I will say it again: our quest to fix ourselves and obtain an identity will inevitably fail. Regardless of how hard we strive to justify ourselves by pursuing our SOSR, it only disappoints and enslaves us. Because we were created as derived identities, we cannot justify ourselves and generate an identity of our own. We need someone outside of ourselves who has the authority to give us an identity, someone who is both perfectly just and perfectly loving, who will never change his mind about us and who will give us an identity. We need a redeemer.

So far in this book, we have looked at what is wrong with us and at the obstacles that lie in the way of obtaining our true identity. In part 2, we will look at what can make us right.

# *Reflection*

Consider how you survived the emotional pain of your past.

1. Did you have repeated experiences of feeling rejected, unloved, hurt, and the like as a child?
2. What did you do to counter these feelings and the associated shame messages you experienced?
3. Was it more important to assert that you were worthy or to hide your flaws?
4. How are your patterns of asserting your goodness and hiding your badness manifesting now in your life?
5. In what ways have you found your strategies to be helpful or harmful to you and others?

# PART TWO

# WHAT CAN MAKE US RIGHT?

# FIVE

# MORE THAN JUST "KNOWING" THE GOSPEL

The majority of people I've seen as clients in my counseling practice have been Christians. Some of them might be considered "young" Christians who came to faith relatively recently. Some were Christians with a long history of faith. Initially when some people come to faith, they believe their past is wiped out. They have this notion that whatever they experienced in the past—their wounds as well as their failures—should no longer have a hold on them. They may even say, "Isn't that what the Bible says in 2 Corinthians 5:17? 'Therefore, if anyone is in Christ, the new creation has come: The old has gone, the new is here!' We are born again and given a new life in Christ. We are a new creation!" That certainly describes how I felt as a "new" Christian.

I grew up in a Christian home, but it wasn't until college that the gospel became personal to me. To know that I am a child of the one and only almighty God who rules over all things was invigorating for me. How amazing! I remember feeling incredibly free, no longer carrying the shame of my past wounds. I had felt like an outsider, striving to belong, never feeling good enough to be somebody. But my personal faith in God had resolved my past angst, and verses like Philippians 3:13–14 confirmed my resolution: "Brothers and sisters, I do not consider myself yet to have taken hold of it. But one thing I do: Forgetting what is behind and straining toward what is ahead, I press on toward the goal to win the prize for which God has called me heavenward in Christ Jesus." Yet while it is entirely true that the moment we accept Christ we are given a new identity and our sins are completely wiped clean—past, present, and future—we are not completely whole at the moment of our salvation. We are in the state of being already saved yet not fully redeemed.

As I've become older, I've begun to notice a different kind of obstacle. I know too much about what *should* be: what is the right way to live as a Christian, how I should feel toward God, and what I should be doing to grow and serve. And my growing awareness of my failure to live up to these standards has often left me feeling like my old self again—never good enough. And this has led to self-contempt, which isn't what a person who has been saved should be feeling. Sometimes, though it seems odd when we first consider it, "knowing the gospel" can keep us stuck in a cycle of striving and keep us from more deeply internalizing the gospel. As both a younger Christian and an older Christian, I used my faith in God as a way to avoid the broken parts of me. And this kept me from receiving more of his healing and from living with more freedom as who I really am in Christ.

When we recognize that the root of our identity problem is being disconnected from God, then it makes sense that the gospel must be foundational to making us right. The gospel is the story of God's grace to humanity through Jesus Christ, and it affirms our value and worth, giving us an identity that is unshakable. We are made in God's image, and God has made a way for us to be reconciled and reconnected to him so that we now derive our identity from him. The gospel affirms our identity, heals our wounds, and frees us from our idolatrous strategies.

So why is it that even after we "know" the gospel, we do not experience the life-altering power of the gospel more fully or more consistently? Why is it that we can know the truth about who we are yet still be so preoccupied with asserting our significance and hiding our flaws?

Before we get down on ourselves and grow discouraged, let us be reminded that internalizing the gospel is a process in which we are becoming increasingly aware of the effects of sin, both personal and interpersonal. We are being redeemed day by day, and this is true of our healing as well. We become more aware of our wounds, our sins, and the brokenness in the world as we continue to deepen our relationship with God. When I pause to think about it, I am grateful that I do not have to see my sins, my wounds, and the brokenness in the world all at once. I do not think I could handle that! Most likely I would be overwhelmed, feeling hopeless and perhaps even resigned to remaining stuck in my sin. It is God's grace that he *progressively* reveals our wounds to grieve, our sins to repent, and our brokenness to accept as we go through the process of internalizing the gospel.

And yet even knowing that this is a process, I continue to ask, "Why do we often not experience the power of the gospel?" After years of observing and interacting with people who say they believe in God, I've met many whose belief in God either didn't seem relevant in their struggle, or it was very relevant but God was not seen as a positive, helpful presence. I would often hear from them that what they heard about God and what they knew in their heads about God was not what they *felt* about God or what they *experienced* with God. This gap, between the head and heart knowledge of God, is a major stumbling block to internalizing the gospel and experiencing God's transformative power, and this led me to conclude that we need more than just "knowing" the gospel.

In this chapter, we will look more closely at the common phenomenon we refer to as the gap between head and heart knowledge of God, and how this keeps the gospel from going deeper into the broken and painful parts of us. We will first look at *why* we experience this disconnect between our head and heart knowledge of God. Then we will look at *how* we can begin to close the gap through new relational experiences.

## FROM THE HEAD TO THE HEART

A fundamental belief of the Christian faith is that we can have a relationship with the living God. However, God is not a physical being whom we can interact with using our human senses. A number of researchers studying the integration of theology and psychology believe that we form mental representations of God. We have head knowledge or *God concepts*, which are the intellectual or theological understandings we have of God. God concepts are easiest for us to access and communicate. For example, when we are asked, "Who is God?" or "What is God like?" most of us can answer these questions fairly easily. We might say, "God is the Creator of the universe" or "God is loving." On the other hand, *God images*—or our heart knowledge of God—are the emotional or relational experiences of God that are stored in our implicit memory. God images operate automatically and out of our awareness. God images are also more difficult for us to access without a time of deeper probing and processing. And our God concepts tend to be more positive than our God images. This distinction—that we are consciously aware of our head knowledge of God but are not consciously aware of our heart knowledge of God—can be helpful in making sense of the head-heart knowledge gap. In relational terms, we know there is a difference between knowing a person and feeling close to a person. This is why we don't decide who we will marry by reviewing academic transcripts and résumés. We spend time interacting with potential marriage partners. Since God is relational, to have a real relationship with God we need to know about him *and* also experience an emotional connection with him.

Our problem is that we can do a lot to know about God—attend Bible studies, listen to sermons, have quiet times, read books—but if we don't look at what our God image is, we may either create a bigger gap between the two or have a hard time making what we learn about God real and relevant to us. In addition, our God image is influenced by our experience of pain because it is correlated to how we view other people. From what we saw earlier, we know that any experiences we have with others that affirm our shame-based identity stick more firmly within us due to our innate shame and longing for acceptance. And what is most striking about these God images—influenced as they are by our experiences of pain and broken relationships—is that we apply them unconsciously and automatically as a lens to make sense of God.

Our ability to make sense of our world is a reflection of how God made us as meaning makers. We take in information from our physical world and form frameworks to make sense of it all. Every day we make countless decisions without realizing it. Researchers call this implicit processing. This is why when we see an octagon, we immediately associate that shape with a stop sign, or why we don't have to keep learning to ride a bike over and over again. Recognizing a stop sign or riding a bike happens automatically without our conscious effort or awareness. Eventually we can enjoy biking without really thinking about it. According to Tim Wilson, a professor of psychology at the University of Virginia, we are faced with around eleven million pieces of information at any given moment, but our brain can only process about forty of those. So our brain creates shortcuts and uses our past knowledge to make assumptions in the present.[1] We have an amazing brain that is wired to take in, process, and store information for fast access when we need it.

This implicit automatic processing of information also applies to people—and ultimately to God as well. As I described in chapter 3, our relational wounds, particularly those from our early childhood which significantly contribute to our core hurts, form templates that we automatically and unconsciously use to make sense of others and God. To put it simply, our brains rely on similar data from our past, assuming that it is as valid as the actual data in the present moment, to make interpretations. So when Emily was met with a boss who was aloof and disapproving, similar to her interactions with her dad, her implicit lens for how she views male figures in positions of authority was confirmed.

Now imagine how Emily might view God. She is likely to see God as distant, demanding, and disapproving, someone who is pleased only when she does the "right" things. With this underlying dynamic playing out in her relationship with God, Emily was driven to do the right things—attend church, serve, lead worship, and make the right choices in dating relationships. However, when she lost her job and her relationship with her boyfriend ended, these experiences confirmed her implicit beliefs that she is not good enough and God is distant and demanding.

The influence of our implicit beliefs is enduring, not only because they operate in our unconsciousness, but because they are held in our bodies as well. We are spiritual beings with physical bodies, but what we experience in the body with our senses feels and seems more real to us. How many times have you wished that God would allow you to hear his audible voice or longed for a visible sign that he is there? Every day we interact with broken people and are continually exposed to brokenness in our environment. God gave us physical bodies, with all their intricate processing and response systems, because we were made to interact, observe, learn from, and influence our environment, and what we experience in our environment matters. These experiences affect our bodies as memories are formed and then held in our bodies as well. All of this means that people who struggle emotionally are not only struggling in their minds; they will likely have symptoms showing up in their bodies too. For example, the way they breathe or sit, how they hold tension in their shoulders, their sleep patterns, and their digestive processes are all telling us something about their emotional states. We should carefully tend to these bodily symptoms just as we do to any mental or emotional symptoms.

Emily could probably sense within a few days that it would be difficult to work with her boss. She heard clues in his voice and saw them in his facial expressions and body language. As she picked up on these nonverbal cues, her anxiety peaked, and Emily felt the tension in her body as she tried to figure out what would help this situation, and her sleep patterns were thrown off. These are all ways her body was anticipating a potentially painful experience based on her past experiences with her dad. When she felt these bodily reactions, she was triggered and felt overwhelmed, and so she worked even harder. Emily's body was telling her, *I am in danger.* And since her brain is hardwired for survival, it went into reactive mode, driving her to try harder and harder. After eight months of this intensity and then six months of searching for a job, her body was worn out. This illustrates how our implicit beliefs, formed in our painful past, are associated with bodily sensations. And the reverse is also true. When these bodily sensations are triggered in the present, they confirm our implicit beliefs—which also cause pain for us.

We need more than head knowledge about God if we want to experience more of the transformative power of the gospel that affirms our true identity. We need to be in an experiential relationship with him. The closer we are connected with God, the more we will know ourselves. But to access and change our implicit beliefs about God, we will need to face our pain, a pain that is deeply buried in our unconscious minds. Ironically, the relational wounds that shaped our views of God need *new relational experiences* in order to change our views of God. This means that the most significant way to help us face our pain and revise our implicit beliefs is having new emotional, relational experiences with other people that contradict our implicit beliefs.

## TELLING VERSUS SHOWING

I've heard it said that the mind can be a scary place; we wouldn't want to go in there alone. It makes sense to me! We are all likely to be hesitant and afraid to explore our implicit beliefs, especially when they come with painful stuff—our fears, our shame, and memories that we don't want to recall.

But knowing we don't have to face it alone lessens the dread and gives us courage.

God knew that we would need many reminders not to be afraid, because there is so much to be afraid of in this life. But his promise to us in these moments is his presence with us. We need a presence—a person, a relationship—to face what is scary and painful. In fact, those who study the effects of adversity and trauma found that being connected to other people is important not only to survive something traumatic but to heal from it.[2] One study conducted after the 9/11 attacks found that survivors who had supportive relationships exhibited fewer symptoms of PTSD and depression and were able to adjust more quickly following the attacks.[3] Adversity and lack of relational connections are what keep people afraid and stuck in their past pain. The presence of supportive and nurturing relationships are what helps people face what they are afraid of so they can heal and change. So in some ways, feeling alone and unseen in great distress can be even more destructive than the actual event of trauma.

Therefore, to help people experience God as a person in relationship with them, rather than just telling people about God, we need to show people who God is by reflecting his likeness. This revises their implicit beliefs about him. Just as the relational experiences in our past shaped our unconscious beliefs about ourselves, others, and subsequently our views of God, we need new emotional or relational information in order to revise these beliefs. We need to repeatedly experience emotional connection with other people that counters our past experiences.

We all long for emotional connection, which we can define as feeling heard, seen, and valued as who we are and experiencing a sense that the other person in the relationship is on our side and will be there for us. When we experience emotional connection in a relationship, it affects how we feel about ourselves and how we perceive others.

When I was a child, not being able to speak the language and feeling excluded reinforced a sense that I was incompetent and didn't belong. Even after I learned to speak English, my sense of incompetence and not fitting in remained, and I often felt that others, both peers and teachers, failed to notice me as a result. Then something extraordinary happened in my seventh-grade English class. Mrs. Macmillin noticed me. Wearing an endearing smile, she said in a warm tone, "Oh . . . I know you. I bet you know all the right answers. I can see the wheels turning inside your head. You don't speak, but I know you are smarter than everyone here!"

In those few seconds, I lifted my head and my eyes met hers. My hunched shoulders opened up and my heart started to race, not from fear, but from delight. I felt seen. I mattered. I felt exhilarated. This brief exchange was so unexpected and out of the ordinary that it remains a transformative moment in my mind. To this day, whenever I feel down about myself, I recall how I felt in that moment. It's not that I believed I was smarter than everyone. Rather, her exchange with me in that moment conveyed, *You are okay as you are. You belong . . . and you have something to offer.* This moment expanded my view of others as well. I knew I was not alone as an outsider. It wasn't me against everyone else. I had a place where I belonged, where people were embracing and caring. This was only a moment, but it became a turning point to help me out of my inner sense of incompetence and the feeling that I was alone without a place of belonging. And it illustrates the power of relationships. When I imagine how God might relate to me, this brief moment comes to mind. I imagine the Lord gazing at me and saying, *You are my beloved daughter. You are mine, and I am with you now and always.* What is exchanged in our interpersonal relationships can rewire our brains to not only revise who we are but also how we see God. These experiences are called *corrective relational experiences.*

In my dissertation study, I found that new relational experiences were necessary to revise how people view God. In that study, the participants described a few key features of corrective relational experiences. First, it is important to establish a *safe space* for people to show their deepest vulnerabilities. This is essential in creating a transforming experience. The safe space is chiefly characterized by *nonjudgmental interactions*, in which any admission of wrongdoing, any perceived weakness, and any character flaws are met with *empathy* and not judgment. Participants noted that they felt *validated* not because their emotional and behavioral responses were perceived as good but because their reactions made sense given the situation and what they experienced in the moment.

For example, in Emily's situation, given her story, it made sense that she felt hopeless, worthless, and ashamed. As these feelings intensified, it also made sense that she would now struggle even to get herself out of bed each day. The focus isn't on whether these responses are good or helpful, or even on fixing these reactions. The focus is on validating where she is at and attuning to what she must be feeling in that moment. Saying something like, "I imagine it must be hard to feel the way you do right now," can be more helpful than saying, "Why are you reacting this way?" or "Cheer up!" This kind of *emotional attunement* is another feature of a corrective relational experience. It simply conveys, *I see there is something going on inside you. Tell me more.* When we experience someone attuning to us, we feel seen, and it is an invitation for us to share more. If Emily receives the invitation to share more, she might say, "I'm so frustrated with myself! I'm not acting like myself right now. I should be job searching and moving on!" For Emily, sharing what is going on internally has not been a common experience. In many of her relationships, she was the one attuning to others. So, for Emily, sharing her own frustration about herself is a good start.

*Curiosity* is another key feature. In general our curiosity about people begets their curiosity about themselves. In corrective relational experiences, our curiosity can be used to help Emily access her painful core hurts and shame messages. Picking up on her frustration toward herself, I might say, "Oh, I hear your frustration. That's heavy. I wonder if your frustration had a voice, what would it say about you?" This is one way to get to her internalized shame messages that can be connected to the painful experiences in her past. As Emily makes connections between her past and her present, those connections will increase her understanding of herself, will lessen her frustration, and may even lead to some empathy for herself.

The final and perhaps most important feature in these corrective relational experiences is articulating the corrective experience that people have had and connecting that experience with God. At some point in our work together, Emily might be able to say, "I'm a mess, but now I feel like that's okay given what I've experienced. I was afraid to tell anyone, but I actually feel more relaxed now—like a heavy weight has been lifted from me—and I feel hopeful." This is the response of someone who has experienced God's grace. She has had an experience of being seen, understood, and accepted. After she has experienced God's grace, we can connect her experience to Christ, who empathizes with her weakness. She can approach him with confidence to receive his mercy and find grace to help in her time of need (Heb. 4:14–16). For Emily, having a tangible experience with another person made God's truth more real and personal. She experienced God as approachable, not distant. She experienced how God gives mercy and grace in her time of need, not judgment and condemnation.

Having briefly described this process of healing and change, it is important to remember that this process is not quick or easy. I had an extraordinary experience with Mrs. Macmillin as a seventh grader that set me on the path to revising my implicit beliefs about myself and other people. However, since then I've had countless more experiences of God's love and grace through others. I've been in long-lasting relationships with family members, dear friends, mentors, and counselors who have modeled Christ's love to me. In these moments, I've experienced what it means to be Christ's ambassador, to reflect and represent him, and to make his invisible presence seen and known. We can be the look of his face, his tone of voice, the touch of his hand. In spite of all that I have experienced, I have to admit that I am far from having owned my true identity in Christ. It is still a struggle! However, being confident of this, that he who began a good work in us will carry it on to completion (Phil. 1:6), we can persevere with hope and progressively internalize the gospel.

## Reflection

Often how we relate to God is more obvious when we are distressed. As you recount a recent experience of feeling hurt or distressed, reflect on the following:

1. In that moment, how did you experience God?
2. Do you naturally seek him out in times of crisis? Why or why not?
3. How do you experience a gap between what you know about God and how you relate to God?
4. Describe a relational experience with a person who has modeled Christ to you. Can you connect that experience with God?
5. Is there a Bible verse you read or a time you can recall when you experienced something similar with God?

# SIX

# GRIEVING AND
# ACCEPTING OUR PAIN

Some of the few movies I watched at a movie theater in my growing-up years were the *Indiana Jones* franchise. Besides being enamored with Harrison Ford, I was drawn to his profession as an archaeologist. In my young mind, I wondered why anyone would go to such lengths, risking one's life to dig for buried treasures. I wondered if anything was worth that much effort, risk, and passion. And perhaps this is how many of us feel about "digging" through our past for long-forgotten, painful memories. We wonder, *why would anyone devote so much effort to go through all that pain?*

Although we often avoid painful past experiences, as if being exposed to them would surely destroy us, I now view them as buried treasures—priceless artifacts worth the effort, risk, and passion. Sadly, there are times when life requires us to tolerate painful experiences. I had to face bullies every day at school as a child, and it was a painful experience I'd rather not remember. However, the impact of those early experiences did not end when the bullies stopped bothering me. And unless I really understand how I was hurt and how my early experiences shaped my way of making sense of life—especially my sense of who I am—I will remain stuck in that pain. The effects of those early experiences will continue to play out in my present life with an accumulated effect, because my past pain will be further exacerbated as I face even more experiences of racial disparity and discrimination living in this country as a minority. My present interpretations have the potential to be severely distorted by my past unprocessed pain, so my reactions today are not just about my present experience. The buried treasures I am seeking aren't just about what we have experienced but are about how we have made sense of our painful experiences. Those are the priceless artifacts we are after.

When our buried treasures are found and carefully, tenderly cared for, these treasures can lead us to deeper healing so that we will be less triggered by our present situations and our responses will be more appropriate to what we are experiencing in the moment. Moreover, since our painful experiences are what cause us to develop and hang on to our idols ever so tightly, alleviating our pain will also help us to relinquish our idolatrous strategies, moving us closer to obtaining a stable identity.

To recap, what keeps us from progressively internalizing the gospel is our implicit beliefs about God that are shaped in our experiences, forming core hurts that reinforce our shame-based identity. These implicit beliefs about God operate hidden from our awareness, but we can begin to shift these beliefs through corrective relational experiences with other people. When we are able to establish a sense of safety in a relationship, we can then explore our pain, which can be transformed into a buried treasure that will help us find healing. In this chapter, we will look at a pivotal process called *grieving and accepting*, a necessary task in moving toward greater freedom from our past and deepening our relationship with God.

## THE PROCESS OF GRIEVING AND ACCEPTING

One of the hardest first steps for many of us is to identify and accept what is broken in us and to acknowledge that life simply hurts. More often than not, we would prefer to find better strategies to continue to keep things buried or acquire a miracle coping skill that will make us invulnerable to pain. Of course, this tendency is tied to our dependence on ourselves. We prefer to be in control, and when it comes to exploring our pain, it invariably means we will feel emotions that may seem out of control. Not being in control is uncomfortable, but losing control of painful emotions is often too scary to face. Our fear is reasonable, and there are valid reasons for our fear. So the best place to start this process is to look at our fear of facing our pain in the safe presence of another person.

Let's begin by defining the process. *Grieving* involves

expressing the entire range of emotions associated with our core hurts—our losses, wounds, and traumas—in words and in tears to help us move forward toward greater acceptance of what is broken in us and toward greater hope for deeper healing. *Accepting* involves a process of acknowledging the reality of what we experienced. Grieving is interrelated with accepting, since to truly grieve we must learn to face what has happened to us and how these experiences have affected us. Grieving and accepting are so intertwined and interdependent on one another that the combination of both forms one process. Similar to the process of internalizing the gospel, the process of grieving and accepting is a cycle. It is not a process that we go through once, but over and over again as our healing deepens.

I've processed many of my experiences as a child adjusting to a new country. Thankfully, I've had family members, friends, mentors, and a number of counselors who helped me put words to my experiences, grieve my pain, and accept my reality. As a result, I felt I had received God's healing for much of what I experienced during that period in my life. More recently, however, I've been struggling with my fear of public speaking. Although I had struggled with this fear since I was a kid, I had gotten better at dealing with it and felt more comfortable over the years. But as my public speaking opportunities increased over the last few years, it started to bother me again. I found myself agonizing over what to say, how to say it, for how long, how fast, and how loud. And I've lost sleep worrying about not being able to pull it off after all my preparation. Three months ago, during one of my group therapy sessions, I realized that my fear of public speaking is closely tied to a particular memory in which I felt terribly humiliated by a teacher in front of my fifth-grade class. I associated being seen with the feeling of humiliation in that moment. Suddenly it clicked for me that whenever I anticipated being in front of people, that fifth grader in me showed up with hurt feelings and the fear of experiencing that shame and humiliation again. Sometimes even the wound that feels healed can play out in our present life, revealing parts of us that still need deeper healing.

## ACKNOWLEDGING WHAT HAPPENED AND ACCESSING THE PAIN

Perhaps for many of us, acknowledging or recalling painful events in our past may not be too difficult, especially those that highlight our resilience and inner strength. We may often hear these stories from our parents or our grandparents, the stories that usually begin with "Back in my day . . ." Rest assured, we all will do this at some point in our lifetime. And when we do this, we are recalling *explicit memories*, which are one form of long-term memory that we can bring to our conscious awareness when we are attentive and intentional. Presenting our stories to highlight the good in us is not bad or wrong. Often these stories contain aspects that glorify the beauty of God's image in us, and we should celebrate and honor this. The problem is when we pay attention to only the good parts of our stories and ignore the others—the more painful ones.

Accessing the pain in our stories is more challenging because of its implicit nature. Specifically, we are interested in the painful emotional and relational experiences stored in our implicit memory that automatically and unconsciously operate in our present situations. One way to access these is to take notice of when they are triggered. For Emily, there are multiple entry points to help her identify her pain. We can start with her admission of her frustration with herself for not performing well enough or not being able to get out of bed. Another way is to take a recent event and unpack it. For example, take what's fresh in Emily's mind, her recent breakup with Dave. As she begins to share the story about her relationship with Dave, she may start with how the relationship began, what Dave did that made her feel he was the one for her, what process she went through to decide to move to NYC, and maybe even how he made her feel about herself. As she continues her story, her tone of voice may shift or we may notice her shoulders cave.

The breakup began with a growing distance between them. Dave had noticed that Emily was distracted when they were together and had said to her, "Is everything okay? You seem like you've got a lot on your mind. It's been some time now that I've noticed that you are here with me but not really here." After Dave shared this, Emily immediately apologized and tried hard to focus on him in that moment. The following week, she put in longer hours so she could spend the whole weekend with him, expecting that they would spend the weekend together as they usually did. She also decided to share with him her distress over working with her boss. She had mentioned it in passing but hadn't shared how hard it had been for her. As the weekend approached, Emily was really looking forward to seeing Dave and even felt relieved, anticipating the support he would give her regarding her boss. But when she called to tell him that she had a completely free weekend coming up, he told her that he had made plans with his friends to take a weekend trip away from the city.

How do you imagine Emily felt at that moment? How do you imagine she made sense of this exchange? Dave did not know or see all that she had done to free up her weekend, how much effort she had put forth to meet his expectations. She had tried hard to please Dave, but her efforts didn't matter. Does this sound familiar? She felt unseen and discarded, confirming the message that she doesn't matter, that she's not enough. And her longing for connection, to be seen and supported, was shattered when he didn't tell her about his plans until she reached out to him. *He doesn't know me or want to be with me* was the message in Emily's mind. This was the moment that started the downward spiral that eventually led to the end of their relationship.

Accessing the pain of that particular experience can elicit a range of emotions for Emily to process. Any images or sensations she can associate with the experience can be explored to access her emotions. Emily may feel *disappointed* that Dave didn't want to know why she was distracted; *angry* that he didn't tell her about his weekend plans as he was planning it; *sad* that he didn't plan to spend any time with her that weekend; *afraid* that he may not be reliable and is like the others in her life—demanding and unavailable. This incident is what I call an *attachment injury* in their relationship. Emily felt Dave violated the expectation that he would be there for her, especially in times of distress, which caused her to feel betrayed and abandoned. As these painful emotions come to the surface, they should be grieved and processed.

## GRIEVING THE PAIN

Sometimes even when we feel a certain emotion, we are hesitant to admit it because we think that it's bad or wrong to feel that feeling. Sometimes we doubt whether we should be feeling what we are feeling. So we exert our mental energy trying to figure out if our feelings are warranted. This is a way our cognitive, rational thinking kicks in as a way to keep our pain buried. We have plenty of ways to do this, such as denial, rationalization, and minimization. These are common defense mechanisms to avoid what we really do not want to face—the painful emotions.

On the other hand, I have also seen folks like Tom, who do not have any trouble admitting how they feel at all. In his early forties, Tom came to see me due to his stress over potentially losing his business. He grew up under similar family dynamics as Emily. His parents often clashed with one another. His mom was detached and preoccupied, but his dad was overly involved in a bad way. He had a temper and would regularly lash out at Tom, saying he was weak and slow, that he would never measure up to be a man, that he would never make it in life, and on and on. To cope with his home life, Tom started drinking at fourteen and tried to stay out of his home as much as he could. Then Tom suffered a mental breakdown at nineteen, and his parents shipped him off to his grandfather's ranch in Texas. Tom eventually got married, but it ended in divorce. As a result, he lost more than half of his inheritance. Then his business partners scammed him out of his portion of the business. Tom was nearly bankrupt, without any family support, and drinking daily to cope.

Acknowledging what happened to him and even accessing his pain was not a problem for him. He even seemed to feel self-compassion for his various wounds and expressed his anger about those who had legitimately hurt him. It seemed he was processing, but he was not really making any progress toward healing or change. He expressed self-pity or blamed others week after week, repeating the same stories, the same hurt feelings, and even weeping over the same pain. It dawned on me while working with folks like Tom that "processing emotions" can also evolve into other idolatrous strategies that keep us stuck in our pain. Processing emotions involves more than venting emotions. In Tom's case, the validation and the empathy from others was all he wanted to feel okay and justified in his current state of being stuck and avoiding responsibilities. Processing his emotions—recognizing, labeling, and expressing his hurts—became a strategy to avoid his fears of never measuring up as a man and to avoid receiving God's healing for his broken sense of self. Unfortunately, Tom was not willing to explore the deeper wounds of his past, and eventually he decided to end treatment.

As we explore what processing emotions looks like in grieving our pain, we should keep two things in mind. First, emotions are not necessarily wrong in themselves, though they can intensify to drive us to act impulsively and hurt ourselves and others. Emotions are part of our image-bearing quality. Emotions can be the window through which we can explore the unconscious parts of ourselves. We can learn about ourselves through the emotions that we feel in certain situations or with certain people. Our emotions also tell us what sensitivities or core hurts we've developed and what happens when those sensitivities are provoked. We can learn what emotions drive us to pursue what we want and what stops us in our tracks. So emotions are informative.

Second, emotions should neither be suppressed nor vented. Both patterns can evolve into idolatrous strategies to deal with our pain. Moreover, as these patterns persist, they will shape the person we become. Those who persistently and automatically suppress can be perceived as hard, cold, and apathetic, while those who only vent their emotions can be perceived as dramatic, overwhelming, and excessively sensitive. Either way, we will remain stuck rather than growing in understanding ourselves.

Our goal in processing emotions is to feel the emotions without letting these emotions control or overwhelm us. In other words, we need to learn to *regulate* our emotions, to monitor and manage our emotional experiences as well as the expression of what we feel. When we are able to regulate our emotions, they will help motivate us and help us to make wise decisions, maintain healthy relationships, and more. Our emotions get dysregulated because something or someone has triggered our pain. A key component in grieving our pain involves this process of unpacking our emotions. Processing our emotions involves *becoming aware of emotions*, being able to recognize the feeling as a feeling. In doing this, we are taking agency over our emotions rather than being passive and just letting the emotion be felt. Processing emotions also involves *expressing our emotions*, putting language to what we are feeling. This also increases our sense of agency over our emotions. As our sense of agency increases, we are better able to regulate our emotions and then *reflect on the meaning of these emotions* and make sense of them.

Take Emily. She's not used to recognizing, much less expressing, her feelings, but she is able to say, "It upset me that Dave didn't tell me about his weekend plans." As her feeling of being "upset" is validated, she can tell us more about what that feels like. "It was annoying. . . . Well, I feel angry that he did that. I feel angry that he doesn't notice what I do for this relationship." As we stay curious about her feelings, she will be able to recognize her feelings of anger, which are associated with this particular incident and beyond. Her anger is the accumulated effect of Dave's lack of acknowledging her sacrifice to be with him. "I've done all this for the relationship, and you can't even tell me about your plans for the weekend!" And her anger comes from a sense of unfairness—"It is unjust that you treated me this way after what I have done for you!" Up to this point, the process can look similar to venting, but the purpose of processing emotions is for greater understanding of the self and forming a more cohesive narrative to this experience, the relationship, and Emily's whole life story.

Once Emily becomes aware of her anger and understands why she is angry, then she can begin to explore her deeper, more unconscious feelings and beliefs. Often, when we follow the emotions that surface, we can access the core hurts and the shame-based messages underneath them. So we begin with validating Emily's anger. Validating emotions does not involve making judgments. It is an act of acknowledging and accepting another person's feelings, even if they are negative or misplaced. It is an act of listening without dismissing, belittling, minimizing, or rejecting the person even if we do not agree with their emotional responses. This is not an easy skill for many of us because we *do* make judgments or feel uncomfortable with certain feelings, perhaps in fear of being "controlled" or overwhelmed by emotions. As a result, sometimes we do not want the other person to feel what they feel. So in response to Emily's anger toward Dave, trying to be helpful, we may vilify Dave ("He's the wrong guy for you. He's immature and selfish"), or we may encourage Emily to forgive and forget ("Be the bigger person and forgive him. Forget about him and move on; he's not worth your time and energy"). Ultimately, neither of these approaches will help Emily grieve or accept what she has experienced, learn from it, and move on.

Let's imagine how we might access the deeper feelings and beliefs as we follow Emily's anger toward Dave. We can validate and explore deeper in a conversation like this:

**FRIEND/CAREGIVER:** "Emily, your anger makes sense given how you feel you've sacrificed so much for this relationship. What's it like for you to be treated unfairly . . . for you to have done so much for the relationship, yet it doesn't seem like Dave sees or appreciates all that you've done?"

**EMILY:** "He didn't see what I had to give up to be with him. . . . He doesn't see me or appreciate me. . . . He left me."

**FRIEND/CAREGIVER:** "Yeah, he didn't see you or
value what you had to give up. What feelings come
up for you as you say that?"
**EMILY:** "I feel the same old feelings—feeling unseen,
devalued, and discarded."

Emily's reflection about her anger gets us to her core
hurts. As these core hurts are named, getting to her implicit
beliefs will be easier.

**FRIEND/CAREGIVER:** "When you are unseen,
devalued, and discarded, what does that say about
you? What messages do you get about you?"
**EMILY:** "That I don't matter. . . . I'm not good
enough. It makes me feel worthless."

The weight of Emily's internalized shame is ultimately
the reason for her current state of being stuck and feeling
hopeless.

Another vital piece of information needed to build a
cohesive narrative is Emily's reflection on why she burdened
herself to accommodate Dave and tried hard to meet his
expectations. This will give her insight about her idolatrous
strategies.

**FRIEND/CAREGIVER:** "I'm curious. I think you are
right that you did do so much for the relationship.
I wonder what made you do that . . . give up all
the comforts of home, transfer from a stable job,
and come to NYC. I also wonder what led you,

when Dave asked you, 'Is everything okay?' to just
apologize and focus on him at that moment."

**EMILY:** "It's all on me to have others love me."

Emily's reflection may reveal that this is what she does to
keep a relationship intact, a pattern that has been repeated
in other significant relationships. Putting it all together, her
core hurts, view of self, and idolatrous strategies form a
cohesive narrative about her experience with Dave and their
relationship, which actually fits the story of her life.

In this case, her cohesive narrative could go like this:
When Dave told her that he made other plans, Emily realized that she was angry at Dave. He didn't see or value all
that she had to give up to move to NYC. He didn't see everything she was doing, even in the midst of her very stressful
job, to prioritize him. He didn't treat her with the same
courtesy in prioritizing her when planning his weekend trip.
He noticed her distraction but didn't care to find out more.
All of this made her feel unseen in their relationship, which
reinforced the message that she is not important or enough,
yet at the same time, her strategy to accommodate Dave and
burden herself rather than asking for what she wanted in the
relationship also contributed to her pain and to the end of
the relationship. Emily can see that her feelings are valid and
that she was mistreated, but she can also see what she did to
contribute to her pain and what she could do differently in
the future, which gives her a greater sense of agency rather
than feeling like she has to be even more cautious the next
time to pick the "right" person to date. In short, she can see
the validity of her anger. This sets her up to eventually move

toward forgiving Dave and repenting of her own patterns that contributed to her pain.

Keep in mind that this is a simplified version to demonstrate what processing emotions could look like, but Emily will continue to grieve and weep over her loss and process her disappointment, sadness, and especially her fear, not only connected to her relationship with Dave but also with her parents. Her admission "It's on me to have others love me" says a lot. Can you imagine a five-year-old saying that to you? How burdensome and lonely this must have been for Emily all these years. Often, when we experience or witness pain, our urge is to stop it immediately. However, it is important for us to face and stay with our pain in its intensity to be able to put language to it and understand the meaning of it. Sometimes there are no words, just weeping, and that's okay. This is one way to express our pain. Sharing this experience, whether it is in words or in tears, is healing in itself. For another to witness and empathize with our pain is a corrective experience that will deepen our healing.

In the process of arriving at Emily's cohesive story, we make connections from her present relationship to her past to help her understand how the relational patterns have formed and continue to affect her. Not only does Emily understand this external pattern, but more importantly, she can begin to see how her situation fits the story of her shame-based identity and how she has tried to fix or redeem herself without God.

As she grieves her pain, Emily will become more aware and accepting of her own brokenness, not letting her flaws define who she is, but seeing how God sees and accepts her as she is. Some people think that acceptance means that we are justifying what is wrong, that it's okay to sin. The truth is that we have already been justified by what Christ has done on the cross. Because we are covered in his righteousness, we are accepted. In accepting our brokenness, we acknowledge that we are not okay—we are broken and sinful, but we trust in the finished work of Christ. Therefore, we will not remain stuck and unchanged.

People are meaning makers. We take information from our environment and form an internal lens to make sense of our experiences early on in our lives. That initial lens then becomes a way to filter the information to form our implicit beliefs, especially about ourselves, others, and God. Getting in touch with our emotions and processing them can get us closer to revising our implicit beliefs. In the context of a safe relationship, corrective relational experiences can create space for the process of grieving and accepting. One key component of grieving is our ability to process emotions, which involves becoming aware of what we feel and putting words to our feelings. To the degree that we can regulate these feelings, we can reflect on them to learn about ourselves and come up with a cohesive narrative of our experiences to further heal and grow.

The process of grieving and accepting is the most critical aspect in helping people deepen their connection with God. We come to him with our painful implicit beliefs— our core hurts, shame-based views of self, and idolatrous strategies. We pour out our pain before him because our emotional bond is strengthened when we can bring the honest, vulnerable parts of ourselves to him. In the next chapter, we will explore what it looks like to encounter God in our pain and what happens to us as a result.

## *Reflection*

All of us can recall events of our past, take stock of them, and gauge the intensity of the fear or shame associated with those events. Sometimes the best way to engage in the process of grieving and accepting is with a professional counselor. Consider your life story and reflect on the following questions to help you decide how you should process your pain.

1. Are there experiences that have significantly altered your life that you've never talked about?
2. Have you had experiences that evoke fear or shame when you recall them? Do you say to yourself, *It's the past. I'm over it.*

If you've answered yes to either of the above questions, pursuing counseling to process your painful memories would be best.

Otherwise, journaling can be a helpful way to process the events in your past. Try to write out your experience and share it with a trusted person who will empathize with you and listen to you. Or write your own psalm of lament to God.

SEVEN

# USING THE
# IMAGINATION TO
# ENCOUNTER GOD

What do you imagine heaven is like?" asked Sam. Sam had graduated from Harvard Business School a few years ago and was on his way up the ladder at a prestigious firm when he was diagnosed with cancer. He had several rounds of treatment with some success but not enough to eradicate the disease. He was only thirty years old, and he was dying of cancer.

I've had many conversations with many different people, but I'll never forget my last conversation with Sam. He was grieving who he would leave behind and everything that was familiar to him. He shared how he would miss going for a run at Central Park and hanging out at his favorite coffee shop with friends. He said how much he wished he could celebrate just one more anniversary with his wife, one more birthday with his friends, one more holiday with his loved ones. He had accepted the reality of his impending death, but to ease the pain of that moment, we imagined together. We imagined heaven—how we will look, what we will eat, what we might say to Jesus, and what it will be like to live for eternity. We wept and we laughed together.

On that day, as Sam and I explored the idea of heaven, heaven was not physically present to either of us, nor was it familiar. We had never experienced it before, but through our imaginations we were able to envision our eternal home and anticipate the joy that would come with being there with Jesus. And for that moment, what we imagined about heaven relieved the sadness of our losses and amplified our hope for what awaits us.

The capacity to imagine is a uniquely human quality, and I believe it reflects God's image in us. Our imagination is generated from within and does not depend on what we can see, hear, feel, taste, or touch in our reality. In my own practice of counseling, I've found that the imagination can be powerfully used to bring relief and healing to people. We can deliberately use mental imagery to visualize desired outcomes—like passing an exam or getting over a fear of flying. We can use imagination to manage difficult emotions and relax our minds and bodies—by picturing ourselves walking on a quiet beach listening to the sound of waves or imagine hearing God's assuring words like, "Do not fear, for I am with you; do not be dismayed, for I am your God. I will strengthen you and help you; I will uphold you with my righteous right hand" (Isaiah 41:10). We can use the imagination to process past experiences through experiential techniques—like the empty-chair exercise where we picture ourselves as a child or another significant figure and speak to the empty chair as if we are talking to that person. After we share our side of things, we move to the other chair and respond to what we just said from that person's perspective, taking on their role. We dialogue with a person who is not present in physical form.

As we saw earlier, we already have an image of who God is in our unconscious mind. This operates automatically, without our awareness. So in these exercises, we are making "real" what is already in our imaginations, interacting and dialoguing with God. We use our imaginations to create encounters with God. In this chapter, we will explore why it is necessary to dialogue with God, what it looks like to interact with God, and consider what the outcome is of having an encounter like this with God.

## WHY WE NEED TO TALK DIRECTLY WITH GOD

When we face our pain and suffering, especially as we go through the process of grieving and accepting, we begin to see the magnitude of our brokenness and feel an overwhelming sense of despair. This often leads to the inevitable question of *why. Why did this happen to me? Why did God let this happen to me?* As we wrestle with the question *why*, we also become aware of the discrepancy between what we know about God and the implicit beliefs about God that dictate how we relate to him. The shift in our implicit beliefs happens as our despair motivates us to *want* what we know about God to be true—that he is a loving God who will never forsake us and who can and will deliver us from our pain.

Just as we don't think about seeing a doctor until something hurts, we tend to see our need for God when we begin to get in touch with our shame and core hurts and as we recognize that our strategies cannot fix what is broken within us. As Emily processed the emotions related to her breakup, she accessed the pain of feeling unseen and devalued and grieved the painful message that she was not important or enough. Not only was this true in her recent relationship, but she realized she's carried the pain of these beliefs about herself throughout her life. She also recognized the futility of her strategies to suppress her pain and of her attempts to set herself free from her shame-based identity. It was God's grace through the working of the Holy Spirit that helped her to recognize all this. The despair and hopelessness of fixing her brokenness led her to want God to be the God of the Bible rather than a God who is distant and demanding. In other words, her pain and crisis led her to want to revise her implicit beliefs about God.

In any relationship, when we have the question *Why did they do this?* we can ponder, analyze, and draw a conclusion by ourselves, but we can't be completely sure of our own conclusions. So we may decide to involve a third party to help us figure out the *why*. This occurs frequently in counseling when a spouse or a parent wants to understand their spouse or child. Once I had a parent share about her twenty-two-year-old daughter's indecisiveness about what to do after graduating from college. The mother mentioned that her daughter had problems taking initiative in a lot of things growing up. As a result, both parents had to continue making decisions for her even in college. They had to monitor her study habits, the amount she was eating, and how she was spending her time. I sensed this mother's love for her daughter, and as a parent myself, I empathized with her distress. She wanted to know why her daughter required so much care at age twenty-two and why she couldn't be more independent.

I said to the mother, "I can tell you care deeply for your daughter, and what you're asking is a good question. I'm curious too. I wonder what she would say about that. Have you asked her?" Now, I could have offered some thoughts based on what she had shared and perhaps provided some perspective about her daughter. However, I think it's good practice not to offer counsel about or analysis of someone who is not in the room with us. So I affirmed her curiosity and her care for her daughter and suggested asking her daughter directly. I may have responded differently if her child was very young, but it seemed to me that at twenty-two, engaging her daughter directly would be the best starting point for clarity and eventually alleviating this mom's distress. As this mom began to address these questions directly with her daughter, she discovered that her daughter often felt paralyzed with the fear of disappointing her parents. She had so much respect for her parents that the fear of letting them down immobilized her. Although they loved and cared for one another, the way they related to each other needed to change. As the parents learned to relax their efforts to protect their daughter, she gradually learned to be less fearful about possible mistakes or failures. She also began to perceive her parents' behaviors differently as her parents focused on being curious about her thoughts and feelings, validating her feelings, and affirming her perspectives.

Similarly, when we have questions of *why* with God, it's most helpful to engage directly with him. In the story of Job, his friends offer their explanations for Job's suffering, but none of them come close to offering a plausible reason for his suffering or really help Job in his time of distress. It's only after Job directly engages with God that he is not only comforted but recognizes his own brokenness (Job 42:1–6). When we engage God directly, the process of pouring out our despair—*Why me? Why now? Why this?*—will be a new relational experience with him that will begin to shift how we relate to him. We can observe this process unfold in the Bible as well, especially in the book of Psalms. As the psalmists pour out their despair, their perception and their experience of God shifts, sometimes by the end of the chapter.

- Notice how Psalm 4 begins with "*Answer me when I call to you, my righteous God. Give me relief from my distress; have mercy on me and hear my prayer.*" And then it ends with "*In peace I will lie down and sleep, for you alone,* LORD, *make me dwell in safety*" (v. 8).
- Psalm 10 opens with "*Why,* LORD, *do you stand far off? Why do you hide yourself in times of trouble?*" In

closing it says, "*The LORD is King for ever and ever; the nations will perish from his land. You, LORD, hear the desire of the afflicted; you encourage them, and you listen to their cry*" (v. 16–17).

- Psalm 13:1 says, "*How long, LORD? Will you forget me forever? How long will you hide your face from me?*" And the psalm ends with "*I will sing the LORD's praise, for he has been good to me*" (v. 6).
- Psalm 22 begins, "*My God, my God, why have you forsaken me? Why are you so far from saving me, so far from my cries of anguish?*" It ends with "*They will proclaim his righteousness, declaring to a people yet unborn: He has done it!*" (v. 31).

When we express our despair directly to God, we experience a change within us. We feel relief from our pain and begin to experience God differently because this process of pouring out our distress is not a religious ritual but a relational engagement, a two-way dialogue in which we express our pain and receive God's comfort.

Another reason why it is important to engage God directly is that he is the ultimate source of our derived identity. He is the only one who can give us a stable identity. Emily needs to hear directly from God that he sees her. She needs to know that he knows her name, sees how anxious she is about not being able to secure a job, and understands how alone she feels not being able to tell anyone about her situation and struggles. She needs to hear directly from God that she matters to him and is precious to him—precious enough to give his life for her. If Emily believes what God says and is able to receive his acceptance of her, then she will internalize the gospel even more deeply, shaping the core of who she is.

## WHAT IT LOOKS LIKE TO ENGAGE WITH GOD

Our imagination is a powerful tool for creating *enactments*, which is what I've described as Emily directly interacts with God. Research has well documented that to change how we perceive and relate to God, we need knowledge of God gained through *experience*.[1] The corrective relational experiences we've had with others will certainly help in imagining our interaction with God. But more than that is needed. Because God came to us in human form as Jesus, and because we have many accounts of how he interacted with people in the Bible—like the woman caught in adultery, Peter after his denial, Thomas who needed physical evidence of Jesus' resurrection, and more—it is possible for us to imagine how he would interact with us. Once Emily's implicit beliefs about God begin to shift, it's important for her to approach him with her shame, core hurts, and strategies for her to personally experience God's compassion and comfort.

One of Emily's experiences that formed her core hurts was her experience as a little girl when her dad demanded that she stop crying. As she recalls how afraid she felt as the conflict escalated between her parents, I might ask her to imagine how Christ felt toward her in that moment. She may imagine him saying, *Don't be afraid. I am here with you.* Or a picture may enter her mind, perhaps a picture of Christ holding her, shielding her from her dad's demands. As she hears these words or sees this mental picture, she undergoes a corrective relational experience with God. Emily can also ask God directly, *Is something wrong with me? Why do I always feel like people don't really love me or want me around, that I'm not enough?* Again, using her imagination, I can ask Emily to listen for God's response. Emily may imagine him saying to her, *I made you with a purpose. I know what it's like to feel that way—like you're not really loved or like you don't really belong. But I love you, you are special to me and you belong with me.* Can you imagine this exchange happening between a father and a daughter? This becomes a bonding moment between Emily and God. Emily is able to hear not only that God sees her pain but that he identifies with her pain because Christ experienced not feeling loved and not belonging here as well. As these intimate exchanges occur and God's true view of her settles deep within her, Emily will experience the power to dethrone her shame-based identity and be affirmed of her identity in Christ. Simultaneously, she will experience relief and joy.

When we feel seen and fully accepted, it is much easier for us to admit our wrongdoings. It is when we experience God's kindness that we can truly repent. We not only feel more at ease about confessing our sins, but we are able to see more of what is wrong with us. Emily can now confess her pursuit of idols to counter her shame-based identity, but more than that, she can grieve and repent of her inclination to rely on herself and use even her faith and good works to suppress her pain and feel good about herself.

The purpose of engaging directly with God is to further internalize the gospel, to increase the congruence between what we know and how we relate to God. These bonding experiences with God help to close the gap between our head and heart knowledge of God. The God of the Bible—what we know about God—becomes increasingly more real to us and more relevant to our lives. This direct engagement with God is what facilitates the deeper heart change as the gospel is further internalized and as we experience the following five *R*'s more and more.

- *RECEIVING* **THE COMFORT AND COMPASSION OF CHRIST.** We realize that we are not alone in our suffering. Christ identifies and empathizes with us (Heb. 4:15). He understands our core hurts like no one else because he experienced them firsthand from the people he was trying to save. On the cross, he also experienced the pain of being rejected by the Father on our behalf, a deep hurt we will never know.
- *REMEMBERING* **CHRIST ON THE CROSS AS OUR SUBSTITUTIONARY SACRIFICE.** We come to understand that Christ, who is God, was disregarded, devalued, and discarded in our place (Isa. 53) to atone for our sins. All our sinfulness and our brokenness is now covered and clothed in his righteousness. The almighty God who rules the universe has claimed us as his very own.

- *REJOICING* **IN CHRIST'S RESURRECTION AND IN OUR NEW IDENTITY.** We come to recognize who Christ is and the reality of who we are in Christ. We rejoice in our new identity and in our reconciled relationship with God. We are his righteous children, reconciled to him (2 Cor. 5:15–21) and now counted infinitely worthy of regard and value by the heavenly Father.

- *REPENTING* **OF OUR SINFULNESS AND GRIEVING OUR BROKENNESS.** We become more aware of our sins and the depth of our brokenness, yet it does not crush us because of what Christ accomplished on the cross. We simultaneously experience the fullness of his love for us. As a response, we can confess our sin and grieve our brokenness without condemning ourselves.

- *REFLECTING AND REPRESENTING* **CHRIST AS HIS AMBASSADORS.** Overflowing with our joy and affection for Christ, we are free to love and serve others and to be a light in the world. We do not seek to do good or be good as a way of justifying ourselves. When the gospel becomes progressively internalized, we want to reflect and represent the one we were designed to image.

Dr. Elena Kim, a psychologist and researcher, led a research team that sought to identify key moments when the gospel message became more real to people. One pivotal moment occurred as people directly engaged with God, confronting him with their questions of why and their emotional pain. Another key moment occurred as people perceived and received God's comfort and compassion.[2]

## SYSTEM OF SELF-REDEMPTION
(What do I need to do to feel okay about myself?)

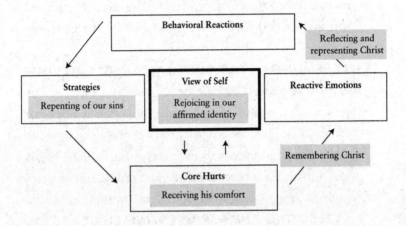

In the account of Emily's experience, we can trace the five *R*'s of internalizing the gospel:

## RECEIVING CHRIST'S COMFORT AND COMPASSION

**EMILY:** "As I was telling God what happened to me and how angry I felt about it, I felt this familiar feeling come over me . . . feeling unseen, like I don't matter. It was difficult to shake off. . . . It felt very true and very real. The more I told God about feeling unseen and how that made me feel, the more I felt like he understood. . . . I mean, he knows what it's like to feel unseen and discarded. I heard him say, *I see you and feel for you.* That made me feel better. God understands me. That helped lift the isolation, and I saw myself in his embrace."

Emily realizes that she is not alone in her suffering and that Christ identifies and empathizes with her. She directly envisions Christ speaking to her and sees herself in his embrace.

## REMEMBERING WHAT JESUS DID ON THE CROSS

In the safety of Jesus' acceptance of her, she can engage with him even more honestly.

> **EMILY:** "Is something wrong with me? I feel like I'm the only one who is this messed up. Why? Why can't you help me? Do you see how hard I'm trying?"
>
> *(Pause as if Emily is listening)*
>
> **EMILY:** "I know what God would say. I feel like I can hear him say, *I made you. You are a mess, but I've got you. Remember the cross.* Then it came to me—he will finish the work in me. I still feel like something is wrong with me, but I don't feel as ashamed."

Similar to the psalmist, Emily's discourse with God can take a turn because she has experienced being fully seen by him and receiving his compassion. As she receives his truth in love, she *remembers the meaning of Christ's death on the cross*, and the reality of who she is in Christ becomes more real.

## REJOICING, REPENTING, AND REFLECTING

God's affirmation that he made Emily with a purpose, that he loves her, and that she belongs with him counters the message of her shame. As her shame weakens, the reality of who she is in Christ is more deeply incorporated within herself. Emily will thus *rejoice in her new identity* established in the strength of her connection with Christ. It's not that she feels she is no longer broken or sinless—she still feels like something is wrong with her—but she does not feel ashamed about it.

When we feel safe in Christ's acceptance and love, we will become more aware of and more willing to own what is wrong with us. In Emily's case, she may become more aware of her sinful patterns of pursuing security through her job and working hard to meet perceived expectations in her relationships with others. She may also grieve her inclination toward her own system of self-redemption to suppress her pain and redeem her sense of insignificance. As a result, Emily will *repent of her sinfulness* in seeking idols and grieve her innate inclination to rely on herself as well as her lack of dependence on God and trust in him. Yet she is able to genuinely repent and grieve without reverting back to her old pattern of constantly condemning herself.

When we experience an encounter with God in this way—receiving his comfort, remembering the cross, rejoicing in who we are in him, and repenting of our sins and brokenness—*reflecting and representing Christ as his ambassadors* flows naturally from our joy and affection for Christ. The meaning of Emily's work and service to Christ will change. What Emily does will not come from a motivation to earn an identity of significance and worth. She will not seek to do good or be good as a way to justify herself, but she will want to reflect and represent the one she was designed to image, to be who she is, her true, unshakable identity.

## WHAT IS THE OUTCOME OF AN ENCOUNTER WITH GOD?

When I was a child, sitting through a worship service was dreadful at times, especially when the sermon went on and on. Still, every once in a while my ears would perk up with interest and my heart would be elated as people from our church shared their testimonies. I loved hearing their stories, especially the climax of a story, that transformative moment when they encountered God and he changed the course of the person's life. These moments reminded me of the experience of the apostle Paul on the road to Damascus and were often dramatic and gripping.

These personal stories, or testimonies, capture an experience with God and solidify it by putting it into words. My research on changing our God image shows that putting words to an experience with God is an important component of solidifying that change. Reflecting on our experiences also promotes healing in our brains. As we reflect on our stories, share our stories, and hear another person's reaction to them, new neural networks are formed that revise our implicit beliefs.[3]

Putting our experiences into words, forming stories to share, and having others respond to them deepens the healing process and promotes ongoing change. When Emily shares the story of her encounter with God, her story will include the same events, but there will be a different twist to the meaning of those events. Her present struggle of joblessness and heartbreak will no longer be the result of not working hard enough, of wrong choices she has made, or of evidence of God's displeasure toward her, but instead they will be seen as God's way of drawing her near to him, to find him, to see him, and to relate to him differently. She will see these experiences as a means of learning to relate to him as a God who delights *in* her over a God who demands *from* her. This shift will also lead Emily to reorient her life purposes and goals because her story is now understood in the context of his bigger story of redemption. She understands that God will use hardships in life to bring her closer to him and to transform her to be more like him. Hardships are now seen as a way to deepen her connection with God. As she draws closer to him and sees who he is, she will also want to be more like him.

When we experience God in a new way, the gospel becomes more personal to us than it was before. This changes us both on the inside and on the outside in ways that others can see. One key change within ourselves is in how we make sense of our experiences. Our implicit beliefs about ourselves, others, and God are revised. We may experience greater self-acceptance. We may become less critical of ourselves and others and be better able to empathize with others. Our tendency to project only our best selves may subside and we will have greater freedom to be real with others. We may find it easier to be vulnerable. Often another important change is our improved ability to regulate our emotions. We may be able to recognize emotions and express them with fewer reservations. We can reflect on our emotions and gain a deeper understanding of what is going on inside of us. As a result, we can reduce our reactive, impulsive behaviors and respond more appropriately to our circumstances.

Our relationship with God and others can also change significantly. When the gospel is internalized more and more, we experience more and more assurance of God's acceptance of us. Spiritual disciplines such as prayer, Sabbath keeping, Bible reading, and meditation now have new meaning. These practices are not seen as an obligation or a way to save ourselves, but rather as a way to connect with God and grow in intimacy with him. We are able to express our view of God in more personal, relational terms, such as, *God is loving and he loves me as I am*, or *I feel safe and secure because he is my refuge and strength*. In addition to changes in our relationship with God, we experience changes in our relationships with other people. We become more able to extend forgiveness to others and more accepting of others' shortcomings. We are able to establish a community of support for the difficult steps of obedience required to end addictive behaviors. We are also able to establish a community for mutual support and growth in our relationship with God.

Lastly, my research revealed that in having an encounter with God, people often had changes in their overall purpose in life. We do not necessarily alter our goals for our lives; rather, the purpose for those goals shifts because God is made relevant to our goals. For example, the goal of becoming a medical doctor no longer is motivated by financial security or status but becomes a way to serve others and reflect Christ in our work. We desire and are able to explore how our faith can be more integrated in our lives.

The outcomes that we observe as a result of connecting with God are certainly attractive, and I wish I could say that once we've obtained them these changes are permanent. Our ability to maintain these changes, to know who we are and be who we are depends on the strength of our bond with our God. Like all relationships, our relationship with God must be cultivated. It does not remain static. God never changes, but our relationship with him must be cultivated because we are wayward and disloyal to him. We suffer from an innate inclination to rely on ourselves rather than depend on him.

In 2005 I first heard Timothy and Kathy Keller give a talk on marriage in which they compared the work of maintaining a healthy marriage to cultivating a garden.[4] I've since applied this insight to my own marriage and have frequently used it in my work with couples. Anyone who has had experience with gardening knows that gardens take an enormous amount of work and attention. It's not like you can just roll out some sod or plant some seeds and then wait a few weeks to harvest your crops. Gardening requires planning and planting, fertilizing and watering, weeding and pruning before you get to enjoy a harvest. Similarly, our relationship with God and our bond with him requires cultivating. The outcomes and changes that we experience will be sustained and grow as we cultivate closeness with him. To put it simply, we need more and more encounters with God to progressively internalize the gospel.

John is a forty-seven-year-old who identifies as a child of God and a recovering alcoholic. He came to know the Lord twelve years ago. He started drinking in high school as a way to escape the pain of his home life and numb his feelings of rage and sadness. He grew up with a father who also was an alcoholic and regularly beat John and John's mom. John remembers feeling rage at his father and how he would calm himself by thinking, *One day, I'm going to get you back for all this. I'll beat your a\*\*!* That day never came. His father passed away while he was in college.

When John was in college, like many of his peers, he drank as part of his social life. Then eventually drinking became his proactive way to ease the pain of his rage, sadness, loneliness, and fears. Unfortunately, his strategy to suppress his pain entangled him, and by the time he was thirty, his life was no longer manageable. He couldn't make it to work or sustain his relationship with his girlfriend. At the urging of his friends, he went to rehab, but he experienced only a brief time of sobriety. After losing his job and his friends, and feeling hopeless about life, he came to church in desperation. Since coming to know the Lord, he has been to rehab two more times and has had multiple relapses. However, at age forty-seven, he has been sober for more than two years now and he has never been so sure about who he is in Christ. He describes his faith journey as a struggle, a wrestling process to absorb the truth that he is worthy of God's love. At first John believed God required him to become worthy of his love, but the more he realized God's acceptance of him because of Christ and that Christ empathizes with his weakness, his yearning to be free from his addiction persisted. John says that many people have helped him to arrive at this place in his faith. He has been an active member of his church, where he experienced God's acceptance tangibly. He has had mentors who showed him how a father loves a son. He has been in group therapy and seen a counselor for ten years. What helps him the most to stay sober now is the image of Christ telling him, *You can do this, John! You don't need a drink. I am with you!* So now he starts the day doing his devotions and imagining Christ telling him, *Fix your eyes on me, the pioneer and perfecter of faith* (Heb. 12:2).

John's story tells us that internalizing the gospel is not a straight upward process, but one that ebbs and flows as we wrestle with ourselves and face challenges in life. The point is that internalizing the gospel has everything to do with who we are because, again, the core of the problem we struggle with is our identity. We are born with a sense that something is wrong with us. Sadly, throughout our lives, the experiences that confirm this message have more and more influence over who we are. But we can't fix our problem of identity on our own. Instead, the good news of the gospel is that Christ gave his life for us, affirming our identity as his masterpiece. Though we are not yet perfect, we are fully accepted and loved by the most powerful, wondrous being in existence. Can you imagine how he sees you? Can you imagine how he feels toward you? He came to us in human form to give us a tangible, physical experience of his love for us. He saw us as worthy of his suffering and death on the cross. When we can see our reflection in his eyes, we can know who we are and be who we are made to be.

In the next chapters, we will consider several possible ways to cultivate our closeness with God to obtain and maintain our stable identity. When couples come in for counseling, it's usually because they're having too many conflicts that have spun out of control. And while it is important to reduce these conflicts, even more than that, I want to help them identify ways to deepen their connection with one another. Changing the patterns they have set, such as their recurring arguments, is much harder to shift than initiating and establishing new patterns focused on doing things to connect with one another. In a similar way, pursuing and deepening our relationship with God will help us gradually relinquish our system of self-redemption.

# Reflection

Reflect on how God fits in your experiences of pain with these steps:

1. Recall a painful memory in your past.
2. Imagine how God saw you and felt toward you at the moment of that particular experience.
3. How does your perception of God toward you formed in that experience shape the way you relate to him now?
4. How do you personally experience God's comfort and compassion?
5. When you confront God with your disappointments and heartaches, how do you imagine him responding to you?

# PART THREE

# INTERNALIZING THE GOSPEL

EIGHT

# LOOKING AT OURSELVES AND KNOWING OUR STORY

E very once in a while I'm asked why I've pursued a career in counseling. And every time I wish I had a better, "holier" answer. The truth is that my interest in counseling began as I became more and more curious about myself. I found myself to be fascinating as I observed what I thought about, how I felt in different situations, how I behaved, how I talked, how I related to certain people, and on and on. I wondered what was going on inside of me and why I did what I did, and that same curiosity eventually led me to wonder about other people as well.

Although I feel some embarrassment admitting that my fascination with myself led me to where I am today, I believe there is merit in self-reflection. Self-reflection is our ability to observe what we think, to get in touch with the feelings associated with those thoughts, and to make sense of our behaviors. Reflecting on what is going on inside of ourselves often leads to more information that connects what we experience in the present to experiences in our past, some of which may remain unresolved and not fully healed. This in turn helps us to organize and expand our story about who we are. Our ability to self-reflect is another image-bearing quality we possess, but it doesn't fix our problem of identity. However, utilizing our curiosity about ourselves is necessary to understand ourselves better, to help us heal and change, and to internalize the gospel more deeply to obtain our true identity.

As we have seen, it is easy to *say* that our identity is in Christ because we consciously believe this is true. But it is more difficult for us to *feel* secure in this identity and live out the reality of who we are in him. We still experience gripping fears, biting worries, a sense of guilt, paralyzing shame, strained hope, hurtful conflicts, and agonizing heartaches. Moreover, our reactions to what we experience are sometimes even more perplexing. I resonate with Paul's words when he says, "I do not understand what I do. For what I want to do I do not do, but what I hate I do. . . . For I have the desire to do what is good, but I cannot carry it out" (Rom. 7:15, 18b). This internal conflict exists in all of us who want to reflect and live out who we are in Christ, and this tension within will not resolve itself completely in our lifetime. Yet there is hope. We can ease the tension as we direct ourselves to internalize the gospel more and more.

At least two obstacles keep us from truly knowing and owning our identity—our *pain* and our *idolatrous strategies*. As I've tried to articulate, the emotional or relational pain that reinforces our innate shame follows us from our past and almost always operates outside of our awareness. Likewise, the idolatrous strategies that we use to suppress our pain and redeem our shame-based identity also operate underneath our awareness. Both our unprocessed pain and our idolatrous strategies powerfully influence our sense of self and worth, but because they influence us without our even being aware of it, they require us to focus and be attentive to ourselves if we want to experience growth and healing. It is like looking into a mirror, meticulously searching and discovering something, and then describing what we see to reflect on it some more. This practice of self-reflection will enable us to move from experiencing to understanding so that we can grieve our pain, repent of our strategies, and make sense of our stories even more.

That said, I want to caution you that the practice of self-reflection is not a one-and-done exercise. It is something that will become a regular practice as you pursue internalizing the gospel and discovering who you are, but self-reflection is not an end in itself. Every good thing can become an ultimate thing, and this is equally true of self-reflection. So be aware of the inclination of your own heart as you practice it.

In this chapter, we will look at a way of reflecting that will help us better understand our pain and our strategies. We will also look at deep idols in greater detail to gain clarity about our primary deep idol. We'll end the chapter by looking at the importance of understanding our stories within the context of God's story of redemption.

## EXPLORING OUR PAIN

Even though we do not like to feel pain, most of us have either experienced or observed that good can come out of adversities, challenges, disappointments, losses, and even traumas. In fact, these can often be transformative. I am reminded again and again as I listen to people's stories that "suffering produces perseverance; perseverance, character; and character, hope. And hope does not put us to shame" (Rom. 5:3–5). As we discussed earlier, our experiences of pain and suffering are like buried treasures that, when they are found and cleaned up, become invaluable gems of wisdom and character. So it is important to do the hard work of exploring our pain.

The unconscious parts of us—the anguish of our wounds and the strategies that we develop to suppress that pain—become more obvious when they are triggered. So one way to identify our core hurts is to reflect on a recent experience in which we felt emotionally upset, lost control of our reactions, became distracted and numb, or lost sleep over it, and then carefully examine it.

A few days ago, I was reminded that I would have to be involved in promoting this book when it is finished. I was told that I may have to do a few interviews or podcasts, and in that moment I thought to myself, *Oh my goodness, what have I gotten myself into?* For several hours, my body felt tense and a pang of anxiety came over me, which kept me from focusing on my writing. I decided to listen to what was going on inside and be attentive to this triggering event.

As I looked inward, I heard the voice of my anxiety waging war in my head. It was saying, *Oh no, you're not really good with interviews and not so good at answering questions on the spot. And you definitely don't like speaking in front of people. Remember that time?* I was recalling my past "disasters." Then it continued, *I don't know if you should have agreed to write this book. Maybe you can still back out of it—you didn't sign the contract yet!*

I've heard this voice before. It was a warning of danger ahead. Just to set you at ease, I'm not actually hearing voices; I'm having a dialogue with myself. My attentiveness to and curiosity about what was going on inside helped me to make sense of why I felt tense and why I couldn't get much writing done that day. Being aware of my core hurts and shame-based identity, I figured this would be related to one of my core fears of being exposed and humiliated. So I asked myself, *What am I afraid of? So what if I am exposed and humiliated?*

The title director of Redeemer Counseling comes with the expectation of a competent, wise, articulate, strong leader. Of course I don't see myself that way, but I've managed to carry the responsibility because I believe God placed me in this role. But this book and what might follow could create a new level of public exposure. And it's not just me at risk of humiliation—I felt that the whole counseling center would be humiliated if I messed up! This was a new level of responsibility I was anxious about. My core hurts of feeling exposed and humiliated therefore kicked up a few notches, provoking my innate shame that said, *English isn't even your first language. You can't pull this off. You don't fit!*

Once again, a new situation that I am facing has triggered the same core hurts and view of self within me. So what *am* I afraid of? That my failing to do my job well would result in ruining not only my credibility but the credibility of the whole ministry. Even though I rationally know that the reputation of the counseling center is not riding solely on my competence, my anxiety has created this narrative. Do you remember my fascination with myself that I mentioned at the start of this chapter? I applied that here, to this situation, and got curious again about why this was coming up for me now. Where was this fear coming from—this fear of not being able to do a good job and feeling exposed and humiliated not only for myself but for someone or something else?

My self-reflection took me back to an incident when I was in the sixth grade. By that time, I was able to speak English better than both of my parents. There was a problem with our phone bill, and I was given the task of calling and correcting the mistake. I remember the weight of the responsibility I felt having to resolve this problem for the family. I had never done something like this before. More than being worried about the call itself, I was afraid I would let my family down. In the end, I was not successful in resolving the issue. I felt devastated. I couldn't take care of this phone bill, but more than that, I couldn't help my parents. My parents didn't say they were disappointed, but I saw their distress. I never wanted to feel that incompetent and helpless again. So I made a vow to myself—*I will pursue competence in things that are likely to succeed. I will not take on respon-sibilities that are too risky.* I vowed to pursue competence and diminish the risk of failure. In that moment, my strategy was further shaped.

As an adult reflecting on this incident, I understand how as an immigrant child I had to be more responsible than my peers for things I regularly felt I could not handle. That similar anxiety was being triggered in my present situation of having to write this book and anticipating what will follow—a responsibility that feels too big for me to handle. In a sense, the pain of my twelve-year-old self surfaced and that sense of incompetence and helplessness overwhelmed me.

My process of self-reflection started with noticing the triggering event and looking inward for an emotion. Mine was anxiety, but that emotion can be anything from frus-tration, to sadness, to confusion. Whatever it is, listening to what it is saying will usually reveal our core hurts and view of self. Then, as we make connections from our past to the present, our understanding of ourselves will expand. My core hurts of feeling exposed and humiliated were closely associated with feeling incompetent and helpless, which I needed to grieve and then receive God's comfort.

## UNDERSTANDING OUR
## IDOLATROUS STRATEGIES

Our stories inform us that there are "good" reasons behind our strategies. Why we numb ourselves with substances, pornography, and gaming to seek comfort; why we pursue career success or accumulation of wealth to have power and feel like somebody; why we go from relationship to relationship, in a never-ceasing search for approval; why we burden ourselves to be "perfect," seeking to control what we cannot in order to feel secure—all of these can be reasons why we feel the way we feel and do the things we do. Understanding our strategies is not the same as justifying them. We seek to make sense of them, not make excuses for them.

As I discussed in chapter 4, most of us can identify the things, people, or pursuits that have become ultimate things in our lives (surface idols). However, the deeper motivations of our hearts are harder to identify. As we recount our stories and pay attention to our responses to painful experiences earlier in our lives, we may be able to discern a pattern that we tend toward, either mastery or avoidant. A mastery pattern, characterized by a deep desire for control or power, tends to assert or seek confirmation that *I am good*. An avoidant pattern, characterized by a deep desire for approval or comfort, tries to avoid feeling exposed that "I am bad." These four desires—control, power, approval, comfort— also have an orientation, meaning that each desire is either directed toward the self or others. The desire for control tends to overload the responsibilities on the self, while desire for power is oriented toward dominating or having power over others. The desire for approval is dependent on others for the approval, while desire for comfort is directed to the self by avoiding responsibilities, stress, and pain. Although we have all four desires, one desire usually becomes more prominent and enduring in our stories.

# STRATEGIES: FOUR DEEP IDOLS

|  | *Mastery* | *Avoidance* |
|---|---|---|
| *Others* | **Power**<br><br>(dominates others) | **Approval**<br><br>(appease others) |
| *Self* | **Control**<br><br>(overloads the responsibility of self) | **Comfort**<br><br>(avoids responsibility of self) |

Returning to my story, as a twelve-year-old I vowed to pursue competence while minimizing the risk of failure. To avoid feeling exposed and humiliated, I sought to be competent at everything I pursued. This also meant that I wouldn't pursue things that I wasn't as good at, so I pursued getting good grades, playing the piano and cello, complying with my parents' expectations for doing chores, and caring for my siblings. I stopped competing in piano competitions when I didn't win first place. I didn't apply to my top choice schools when I didn't do as well as I wanted to on my SAT. My surface idols were grades, being proficient in music, and meeting expectations. But my deeper idol was control. I clearly exhibited a mastery pattern, pursuing a sense of competence and self-worth by doing. Between power or control, I preferred control because I put the pressure on myself. I know that my strategy of control developed long before the sixth grade, but in this particular moment my strategy became more defined: I would only pursue competence in things I was good at.

As we get older, life gets more complicated, and our strategies become more sophisticated. I wasn't aware that this particular strategy was tied to a painful experience in my past until it was triggered a few days ago. As long as my strategies are working, I wouldn't have to feel the pain of my core hurts that aggravate my shame. So was this experience something good for me? Some might say no, questioning what value there is in dredging up past memories. But remember, like finding buried treasures, strategy failures like this are opportunities for us to know more about ourselves, to heal and grow.

If you are curious about what your preferred deep idol might be, reflect on the following statements and identify which set of statements describes you best. Then refer to the key at the end of the chapter to identify your deep idol.

## *Deep Idol 1*

1. I pressure myself to do more or burden myself with more things to do.
2. I feel anxious about having too much to do.
3. I feel worried when I can't be certain about something.
4. I feel guilty and often blame myself for not meeting others' expectations.
5. I condemn myself for not performing well enough or doing enough.

6. I try not to burden others and don't like to ask for what I need or want.
7. A sense of security, stability, and certainty is most important to me.

## Deep Idol 2

1. I am motivated for success and like to win.
2. Getting respect from others is important to me.
3. Having the capacity to influence others is meaningful.
4. My greatest fear is humiliation and feeling insignificant.
5. I frequently feel frustrated and annoyed at other people's incompetence.
6. I expect excellence from others.
7. When something bad happens, I seek out who is at fault.

## Deep Idol 3

1. I crave connection with other people and seek to connect with many people.
2. I feel unsettled if I think someone is upset with me.
3. I have trouble following through on commitments because I tend to overcommit to people.
4. My greatest fear is rejection from others.
5. I avoid interpersonal conflict.
6. I seek to be liked by other people.

7. It makes me happy to see other people happy with me.

## Deep Idol 4

1. I value feeling free and avoid having to feel too responsible.
2. I don't mind spending a lot of time by myself.
3. Privacy is important to me, and I don't like or seek accountability.
4. My fear is feeling stressed and having too many demands on me.
5. I don't dislike people, but I also don't care deeply for them.
6. I like to do what is fun for me.
7. I often feel bored and struggle with feeling apathetic toward others and about life.

Having read through these statements, you may become more aware of your tendencies and which desire within you is likely to dominate. More than knowing which exact deep idol is playing out in certain situations, what is most important is that we understand that there are deeper motivations or desires that evolve into demands within us. If and when your deep idols become clear to you, you will be able to grieve more deeply because you will understand why a specific desire became dominant. You will also be able to repent of your underlying desire and the object of your desires more specifically.

Once we have identified the core hurts that personalize

and reinforce our innate shame and our idolatrous strategies, we have done the hard work of uncovering what is unknown to us. Our story of who we are is becoming clearer, but our self-reflection isn't complete until we reflect on how our stories fit within the context of God's story.

## OUR STORY WITHIN GOD'S STORY

Have you ever asked yourself, *Who am I?* or wondered, *What's the meaning of my life?* Why are you here? What's your purpose? In psychology we refer to this as the existential angst that we go through because we feel lost, living without meaning or purpose, without a sense of who we are or a sense of worth. I think many of us can relate to this existential angst, especially in times of personal hardship when the world around us feels more chaotic and hopeless. However, this existential angst really started the moment sin entered our world and separated us from God. It's present at our birth and gets triggered in different seasons of our lives.

Because we are beings created to derive our identity from God, the most important aspect in the practice of self-reflection is understanding our stories within the context of God's story. In counseling what we often do is help people get clarity about what is happening internally for them and then put the pieces of their experiences together to arrive at an organized, coherent story of their life and who they are. This is helpful to us because we are wired to make sense of ourselves and to find meaning and purpose in our lives.

However, it's not enough to only know our own stories, because ultimately we cannot fully know who we are, why we are here, and the meaning of life without understanding God and his story.

Our life stories did not begin at our birth. We were a part of God's plan before we were knitted together in our mother's womb. In Genesis 1, we read that Adam and Eve are the climax of God's creative activity. He placed them not in an unformed, unfurnished setting to survive in, but made sure everything was set for them to live with purpose and meaning and be fruitful as his image bearers. Then God saw all that he had made and declared that "it was very good" (v. 31). In God's story, he delighted in what he created. He didn't create us out of necessity; he made us out of his sheer delight and gave us an identity, purpose, and meaning.

When I imagine what God's delight might be like, my own dad comes to mind. He delighted in giving us, his three kids, food experiences. I always loved and looked forward to his cooking. For my dad, it was about more than food; he loved the experience of watching us feasting on what he had made for us. I will never forget the first time he made us hot dogs. He said, "Today I'm going to make you an American dish, and you are going to love it!" I waited in anticipation until finally the hot dogs were ready. The amount of food was just as important as the taste for my dad. I remember the large hot dog he served us, wrapped in a sizable bun with ketchup, mustard, and a heap of sauerkraut. My dad, with his eyes open wide, waited for us to take a bite. As soon as we responded, "Yummmmm!" he smiled from ear to ear with an expression of satisfaction and sheer delight on his face. To this day, it's unforgettable in my mind. That's the expression of delight God has for me!

Just the fact that God created us out of his delight says volumes about who we are. But his delight did not end when sin severed our connection with him; he already had a plan to reclaim us. It was for the joy set before Jesus that he endured the cross. We were worth it to him to set aside his glory, come to us in human form, suffer and die on the cross for our sins—all of it: past, present, and future. Now we are clothed in his righteousness! We hear this truth, but we also need to pause and reflect on what this means. It means that though we lie, cheat, steal, gossip, slander, hate, lust, envy, boast, and commit all kinds of sin, yet we are clothed in his righteousness. Regardless of what we do, no matter how broken we are, we are counted as righteous! We can know even now that he is pleased with us and hear him say, *You are my beloved child in whom I am pleased.* This is the identity we have in Christ.

However, even though I firmly believe my identity is in Christ, when something unexpected and hard happens to me, my first thought is, *What did I do wrong?* It's as if there is a formula I need to follow to avoid any hardships and have a peaceful, thriving life. And this is why I need to be reminded of God's story again and again. In God's story, even though we are who he says we are and are clothed in his righteousness, we are not yet perfect. God is in the process of redeeming us and redeeming all of creation. So even if we do everything right, we will still face adversities, challenges, diseases, and heartaches. However, when we know who we are in him, we will make sense of our suffering differently.

Remember that it's not what we experience but how we make sense of it that makes all the difference. In God's story, there is new meaning and purpose in our suffering.

In God's story, we know that suffering is not meant to punish us or a sign that God doesn't care about us, but we understand that he draws us closer to him through it. He tells us that suffering will make us stronger, wiser, and better at reflecting and representing him. Along with a change in perspective, God's story renews our hope because what he promises in this life is his presence with us and the indwelling power of his Holy Spirit. We begin to find our story in God's story.

As we practice self-reflection, we will see more of the pain that we need to grieve as well as more of the idolatrous strategies that we need to repent of. Our stories will expand and be revised with more key details that make better sense of why we are the way we are and why we act the way we do. Yet, at the same time, these new insights about ourselves should not end with just a better, more cohesive story centered on us. Our stories must be expanded and revised within the context of God's story. When we are able to see our stories within his, we are reminded of his truths and they sink deeper into our hearts. We better understand who we are in Christ, which gives new meaning and purpose to our suffering and renews our hope.

# Reflection

Reflect on how you have tried to find an identity and suppress your pain (or how you have utilized your idolatrous strategies).

1. Name the person, object, or pursuits that have become more important to you than God (surface idols). Identify your dominant deep idol. How do you make sense of why these idols became so important in your life?
2. Notice the feelings that come up for you as you name your idols. Tell God about what you are feeling: regret, guilt, shame, etc.
3. Remember Christ's righteousness that covers you—the Bible tells us that "God made him who had no sin to be sin for us, so that in him we might become the righteousness of God" (2 Cor. 5:21).
4. Express your gratitude to God using these words: "I delight greatly in the LORD; my soul rejoices in my God. For he has clothed me with garments of salvation and arrayed me in a robe of his righteousness, as a bridegroom adorns his head like a priest, and as a bride adorns herself with her jewels" (Isa. 61:10).

5. Be affirmed in your identity as the Bible says
   that since we are his children, we are his heirs.
   In fact, together with Christ we are heirs of
   God's glory (Rom. 8:17).
6. How do you make sense of your story in the
   context of God's story?
7. How has your narrative of why you experienced
   pain shifted as you explored your story within
   God's story of redemption?

**(Deep Idol Statement Key: 1 = Control; 2 = Power;
3 = Approval; 4 = Comfort)**

# NINE

# CONNECTING
# WITH OTHERS

During a speech at my daughter's convocation ceremony, I heard a quote by Maya Angelou: "People will forget what you said, people will forget what you did, but people will never forget how you made them feel."[1] The quote captured my attention, and it got me thinking that I don't *want* people to forget what I say or do, but both my experience and research seem to indicate that Angelou's statement is very true! People are more likely to remember how I've made them feel than anything I say to them or do for them.

This goes back to how we are made, as people who derive our identity—who we are—from outside of ourselves. Having lost connection with God, who is our primary source of identity, we not only live with internalized shame, but we carry a deep longing to be known and accepted. Even though we all have this longing, our innate shame makes it hard for us to be transparent, to really be known by others, because if we are not accepted as we hoped, the shame that invokes in us may be unbearable. In our effort to be accepted, we strive to show what we perceive to be good and hide what we perceive to be bad about us. The problem is that when we do this, even when we are "accepted" we don't feel like we are fully known.

The longing inside of us is blocked because of our innate shame, but shame, as pervasive as it is, cannot withstand grace. When shame is met with unmerited grace, it loses its power to define who we are. This is why we have to continuously push the gospel of grace into ourselves so that it changes the core of our identity. Just as the practice of self-reflection helps us target the deeper messages of shame to grieve and to repent of our ways of resolving that shame, the practice of connecting with other people can help us experience what we lost in the garden—being naked but not ashamed—the sense of being fully known and fully accepted. The truth is that this longing will only be completely fulfilled in heaven. However, since we are spiritual beings with physical bodies, what we experience with our human senses can help make God's truth more real to us even now.

When I first came to Redeemer Presbyterian Church in 1998, I didn't come to hear exceptional gospel preaching or to be part of a vibrant gospel community. I came because my husband (who was a pastor at the time) and I were "kicked out" of the church we had been serving in. We were completely distraught, feeling betrayed by the senior pastor we had considered our spiritual mentor for more than seven years and feeling utterly lost about the direction of our lives. We wondered, *Do we continue in ministry, or do we find secular jobs? Do we move out of New York City? Do we go back to school? Go back home?* In this unsettled, emotionally distressing, and spiritually wounding period of time, I believe God led us to Redeemer to experience his grace through community. We joined a small group who embraced us with love and prayer. One of the first things we had to do was move out of the apartment that had been provided for us by the former church. Cut off from the community that we had served, my husband and I were left alone to tackle the work of moving out of our apartment as soon as possible. Our small group leader volunteered to help, and fortunately he looked like a strong guy. He rode with us in our rented U-Haul truck, helped my husband load our things, and moved us into our new place. He barely knew us, but he showed us great kindness in that particular time of need. It felt like such unmerited favor. Then he and his wife continued to show us God's grace in tangible ways by inviting us to meals where they listened to our story of rejection and betrayal and empathized with our pain. They were there when we needed somebody to be there for us, and we felt seen and heard by them.

What we experienced with them was *emotional connection*: the experience of feeling heard, seen, and valued as we are, and a sense that they were there for us in our despair. When we experience emotional connection in a relationship, it affects how we feel about ourselves and how we perceive others. For example, when I experience feeling loved, I see myself as worthy of love and see others as capable of loving.

When this becomes a repeated experience, I will start to believe that I am lovable and others are loving. Our experiences of emotional connection in relationships not only shape but also revise the implicit beliefs we have about ourselves and other people. This is the power of relationships!

Being relational beings, we were made to derive our identities outside of ourselves. We were meant to connect with others on an interpersonal, emotional level and experience being known and accepted. But don't take my word for it. There is plenty of empirical support indicating that strong, fulfilling relationships help people maintain not only their emotional health by reducing stress or anxiety but also their physical well-being. In a 2010 review of 148 studies, researchers found that social relationships improve lifespans.[2] People in healthy long-term relationships are 50 percent less likely to die prematurely than people without them. In addition, we now have even more data confirming the importance of emotional connections, not only in the healing process after trauma and adversity but also in developing our ability to regulate our emotions and build resilience. According to trauma care experts, our capacity to heal from trauma is primarily dependent on our connectedness to other people.[3] Being with people who are present, supportive, and nurturing and having a sense of belonging are crucial in our ability to manage stress and heal from adversities. From a developmental perspective, children with strong bonds with their caregivers, who have had predictable, moderate challenges in their upbringing are more capable of demonstrating resilience in the face of adversities than those who did not have strong relationships with their caregivers. Both our healing and our health are directly correlated to our connectedness with other people.

It has long been established that the single most crucial element in effective counseling is the strength of the relationship between the therapist and the patient. I find this information both relieving and humbling. It is relieving to know that I don't have to be an expert who knows everything to help people. But it is humbling to know that while I can have all the knowledge and skills needed to help people, without love those things are ineffective. As 1 Corinthians 13:1 says, "I am only a resounding gong or a clanging cymbal." As beings made for relationships, we are designed to need experiences of grace and emotional connection. So our longing for connection makes sense. However, this longing coupled with our internalized shame makes us fearful and hesitant. As much as we long for connection, connecting is scary because we unconsciously know that we are not acceptable. This fear in us makes it difficult to find a safe relationship to be vulnerable in and to share what we are going through and receive the grace that we long for.

In this chapter, we will look at how to create and develop emotional connections through the practices of vulnerability and listening, which in turn will help us revise our view of self and bring us closer to God.

## PRACTICE VULNERABILITY

About ten years ago, I listened to a TED Talk on vulnerability by Brené Brown. The talk went viral, and I imagine many of you may also have heard it.[4] In her talk, she not only highlighted the need for connection with one another as beings made for human connection, but also named our shame and fear as the underlying barriers to our ability to feel connected with others. She argued that what is required for connection is vulnerability—to be seen as we are—but because we do not see ourselves as enough or as being worthy, we avoid being vulnerable. I don't know what Brown believes, but I believe Brown's research was homing in on a key aspect of what we have lost as a result of sin—the experience of being naked and yet not ashamed, what she calls vulnerability. We long to be known and accepted, to experience emotional connection in relationships. And to experience emotional connection, we need to embrace our vulnerability and be willing to show the parts of ourselves that we strive to hide. Brown observed that vulnerability takes courage. Deciding to reveal what we've been hiding is very scary. We could be opening ourselves up to additional feelings of shame and inviting all kinds of judgments against us.

In fact, this describes how I felt growing up. After my first experience of being physically attacked by the neighborhood kids, I remember telling my parents, "I'm scared. I want to go back home to Korea." My siblings joined me in trying to convince our parents, but needless to say, it didn't work. My parents consoled us, and after a time of weeping together, my dad instructed all of us to hide our fears. He said to us, "Don't show them that you're even a bit threatened by them. Look them in the eye, and don't let them think you're afraid. Otherwise they will see you as weak and attack you even more. Show them that you're strong, that you're not afraid."

Many of us hear these kinds of messages growing up. And for me, this was the start of learning to hide my fears and what I perceived to be my weaknesses. From that point on, I associated being vulnerable with weakness and feared that if others discovered my weakness, they would take advantage of it. Vulnerability is something I had to learn and then practice, and it still takes a lot of effort for me to openly share my fears, worries, and sadness with others. Yet vulnerability is vital to connect deeply with others. So where do we get the courage to open up?

We should first note that courage is not the absence of fear. In fact, courage is most necessary in the face of fearful situations, when we are actively afraid. That said, it makes sense that we would be hesitant to take risks and open up to others, because the risk is real. We are opening ourselves up to potential judgments that confirm our internalized shame, and that is painful. So it is natural to feel afraid. But the presence of fear can also be an opportunity for us to demonstrate courage. Even more importantly, we must recognize that courage is not something we can generate within ourselves unless we are *certain of who we are*. Unless we know that we are fully known and accepted by God and clothed in his righteousness, it will be difficult for us to take the risk and be courageous. Only as we remember who God says we are will we receive the courage we need to face our fear and take the risk.

And the risk is well worth taking for at least three reasons. First, the very act of taking the risk and showing our vulnerability means that we have taken hold of who we are in Christ. Without his assurance that we are his treasured possession and delight, it will be too scary for us to reveal what we think we should hide. When we are affirmed of our identity in him, we are able to move against our fears and be courageous in showing more of ourselves to others. In essence, in that moment of courage we are internalizing the gospel more deeply. We are demonstrating the truth of who we are by *being* who we really are with others. Our ability to be vulnerable is both a confirmation of who we are in Christ and a way to deepen our identity in him.

Another benefit of taking this risk is that even criticism presents an opportunity for growth. When we open ourselves up to others, we must also expect judgments from others. People will make interpretations of what I share and make judgments about my story and about me. And some of these interpretations may be way off. Remember Job's friends and how they interpreted his suffering? Still, whether the judgments are positive or negative, other people's perspectives can be helpful. Several years ago, a colleague at work told me I was hard to approach and that some folks (including him) were afraid of me. I thought to myself, *How is this possible? Why would anyone be afraid of me?* Perplexed and a little hurt, I went to my trusted source for honest truth, my husband. After empathizing with my bewilderment, he said to me, "Well, it's not that you are unkind or say the wrong things. You just give off this vibe that says, *Don't bother me. I'm busy!*" He went on to tell me that I wear a fierce look most of the time when I'm not directly engaging with people. Apparently I have the same look whether I am focused on a task, stressed about something, or angry at him. Although I didn't like hearing that I have a fierce look, this feedback helped me understand why people found me unapproachable. My husband was able to help me see what I could not see. And my colleague's vulnerability with me led me to examine why and discover a perspective I didn't have before. So other people's perspectives can challenge us either to expand or revise our perspectives, or they can confirm and strengthen our perspectives. How we make sense of things always needs to be challenged and validated because we all have our own implicit lens for making our interpretations.

Lastly, just as my colleague's vulnerability led to my growth, our vulnerability gives us opportunities for others to see themselves in our weakness. They can realize that they are not alone in their struggle and gain courage to be vulnerable themselves. Perhaps this is the counselor in me, but I am drawn to weakness. When people share about their pain, sin, struggle, and suffering, they seem more real to me, more like me, and I feel more connected to them. Every one of us shares a common experience of shame. We all are wounded, grieved, worried, and damaged. So when we share, we are simply reconfirming what we already have in common, the hardship of human existence.

People often bond over what they have in common. The longevity of Alcoholics Anonymous is an example of this. In AA meetings, it is the common struggle and desire for sobriety that draws people together week after week, offering each other grace for failures and celebration of victories. However, I don't believe we need to have experienced the exact same things to connect in this way. Remember, it's not so much what we've experienced but how we've made sense of those experiences that matters. We can connect at a deeper level than our specific experiences. We can connect at the level of our core hurts, shame messages, desire for acceptance, and failed strategies. I don't know what it's like to have been abused as a child, but I can relate to feelings of being defective and not good enough. I can connect with the experience of their pain.

Vulnerability is not weakness; rather, it's an indication that we have the strength to face our fear. When we are weak, we are strong, meaning we have internalized the gospel more deeply and can live out of the reality of who we are in Christ. Yet as much as we want to encourage vulnerability, we must also be mindful that something good can be done in the wrong way or for the wrong reasons. So keep the following guidelines in mind as you practice vulnerability with others:

- **CONSIDER WHAT YOU WANT TO SHARE.** Avoid *over*sharing for the sake of being vulnerable. It is often the things that we want to *hide* about ourselves that we need courage to share, not the things we want to "vent" to receive affirmation or attention. If you do not experience real growth from vulnerability— greater confidence in your identity in Christ, gaining new perspectives and growing in wisdom, and ministering to others through your weakness—then it may be best to involve a professional counselor to help you explore why.

- **CONSIDER WHO YOU ARE SHARING WITH.** We've discussed the risk that comes with vulnerability, but we are also given wisdom to discern who is safe and who is not. Again, vulnerability is not something we practice for the sake of practicing it. Often the risk may be too great if we decide to share with someone we have had difficulty connecting with or someone who has harmed us in significant ways in the past. So we should discern who would be a safe person to be vulnerable with.

- **LEAD WITH SHARING YOUR FEAR** or how you are feeling about what you are about to share with others. When you've considered the previous two guidelines, sharing what is going on for you in that moment can be the start of how you practice vulnerability and may also help you ease into what you want to share. For example, Emily might say something like this: "I'm not used to sharing about my struggles. I've always been able to take care of myself. So this feels strange. I feel a little nervous about telling you, but I don't want to hide anymore. I'm not working right now. Actually, I lost my job six months ago, and Dave and I broke up a few weeks after that."

- **ASK FOR WHAT YOU NEED.** Vulnerability is challenging for us. If you have found a safe person or group to be vulnerable with, then it is safe to ask for what you need in the moment—a prayer, a hug, or assurance that they still love you. Emily might say, "I don't want you to feel sorry for me or anything. I just need to know it was okay for me to share what I shared."

For Emily, it was not okay for her to be vulnerable as a child. So she needs assurance that it is okay for her to be vulnerable now.

Emotional connection is what happens in relationships. It is the dynamics of what is exchanged between people that creates the emotional bond. Practicing vulnerability can initiate emotional connection, so how we respond to others who are opening up to us is just as important. One way we can deepen our emotional connection with others is by listening and learning to respond graciously as we listen.

## PRACTICE LISTENING

In chapter 5, we learned that we can help people experience the gospel through incarnational ministry, in which we model Christ in the way we relate to them. My research has confirmed that repeated experiences of emotional connection may change the structure of the brain to revise our implicit beliefs about ourselves, others, and ultimately our view of God. When this shift happens, the truth about God and who we are in him becomes more real to us. That's why how we interact with people can impact their relationship with God. We can model Christ in many ways, but one key phrase in Scripture comes to mind that has guided me in engaging with others: "be quick to listen, slow to speak" (James 1:19). Listening attentively and actively is one significant way in which we can foster emotional connection with others.

When I was starting out as a counselor, I felt pressured to have something profound to say to my clients. So even though I was trained to understand the importance of listening, I found my mind wandering, thinking about what to ask next or what to say in response to something that was said. I soon realized that it takes enormous intentional effort to listen well. To make it even more difficult, we know that communication is more than just spoken words. Much of communication is nonverbal, which means we also have to observe nonverbal cues. To listen well and really connect with a person, we not only need to listen to their spoken words but must also be attentive to their facial expressions, tone of voice, how fast or how loud they are speaking, the rhythms of their breathing, how they are sitting, and the movements of their body, as well as be attuned to their inner world in order to respond in such a way that they feel seen and heard.

Knowing all that listening entails, doing it well may feel a bit intimidating. We can simplify it this way: *listening attentively is our effort to enter their world and be present with them.* Having the *desire* to be attentive and present is more important than actually being able to do it flawlessly. It is a skill that is sharpened through practice. We may not be able to listen perfectly all the time, especially on days when we are distracted by things going on inside of us. When practicing vulnerability, the focus is on what is happening internally for us; when we are listening, the focus is on the other person and imagining what their inner world may be like. More than insights, coping skills, or potential solutions to their "problems," the best gift we can give to another person is our presence, our willingness to be with them in their struggle and despair.

While listening, we can embody responses that my study has shown to be conducive to facilitating emotional connection. Our responses should be characterized by these five traits:

1. **TAKING A NONJUDGMENTAL STANCE.** Remember our longing and our shame. We all are looking for a safe space to be "naked and no. ashamed," but we have innate shame that tells us we are not acceptable. It is scary to show aspects of ourselves to others. At the same time, we are also interpreters making sense of our experiences, making it challenging for us not to judge what we see, hear, and experience. So recognize that it will take intentional effort to suspend our judgment and listen. One thing that has helped me is recognizing that I don't know everything and thus engaging my curiosity about the other person. Rather than going to the place of judgment, be curious about the other's experience, their story of what happened to them, and how they make sense of what they experienced.

2. **EMPATHIZING WITH THEIR EXPERIENCES.** Because we are relational and social beings, when we are around people who are hurting, we will feel it too. This is why at times we are reluctant to see a friend who is depressed or who has lost a loved one. Empathy is the ability to sense other people's emotions, coupled with the ability to imagine what

someone else might be thinking or feeling. It occurs when we can put ourselves in someone else's shoes and feel what that person is feeling. The ability to empathize with another person's emotional experience is crucial to creating an emotional connection. In response to Emily, I might say, "Emily, I'm so sorry that you had to struggle alone for so long. That is so hard. I'm glad you've shared that with me now."

3. **VALIDATING THEIR EXPERIENCES.** This is similar to empathizing, but it's less about emotions and more about people's stories. People want assurance that their experiences—the way they made sense of them and their responses to them—are valid. Remember that people are trying to make sense of their stories. So, as you listen, try to validate what makes sense to you. With Emily, I might say, "Oh, it makes sense that you would want some assurance that it's okay to share what you did, that you would feel nervous. You are used to handling things on your own."

4. **EMOTIONALLY ATTUNING TO THEM.** Also related to empathizing, emotionally attuning is our ability to recognize, understand, and engage with someone's emotional state and nonverbal cues. So even if someone says, "I'm fine," we are able to recognize when they really aren't fine. We can make attempts to dig a little deeper to find out what's going on. I might say, "I hear you saying that you're fine, but I am wondering if you are really okay. How are you doing?" Or I might say to Emily, "I imagine you must have felt so lost and so alone for the last six months." When we

emotionally attune to others, it helps them to look inward again and be curious about themselves.

5. **BEING CURIOUS ABOUT THEM.** Remember that we all want to be known. So when we are curious about others, our curiosity becomes an invitation to share more. Our curiosity initiates others' curiosity about themselves. We can ask open-ended questions or clarifying questions. We can also simply say, "Tell me more about how you're doing."

In describing these traits, I've given some examples of what you can say to encourage an emotional connection. However, we also need to be mindful of our nonverbal communication. Our tone of voice, facial expression, and eye contact should also be attuned to how the other person is feeling. Remember that our nonverbal communication has a more enduring impact than our spoken words.

In recent years, it has become even more challenging for us to create emotional connections as we see fewer people in person and become more accustomed to connecting virtually through devices. As a society, we are at risk of more disconnection and increased loneliness. So, all the more, we should not give up meeting together and encouraging one another (Heb. 10:25), remembering that new relational experiences that create emotional connection can effectively change our implicit beliefs about ourselves, others, and ultimately God.

# *Reflection*

Our experiences in human relationships both influence how we relate to God and revise our heart knowledge of God. God uses human relationships to help us internalize the gospel. Consider your practice of vulnerability and listening.

1. Identify things about you that you do not want anyone to know. What is your fear in sharing with others?
2. Share your fear with someone you trust who will not judge you.
3. Assess your own listening skills or ask someone close to you about your ability. What do you do well, and where do you need to grow?
4. Imagine how God feels about the things you want to hide. What would God say to you about you? He may say:
   - *Don't be afraid* (Isa. 41:10).
   - *You are not condemned* (John 8:11; Rom. 8:1).
   - *Come rest in me* (Matt. 11:28).
   - *You are my delight* (Ps. 18:19).
   - *You are my chosen* (John 15:16).
   - *I made you* (Ps. 139:13–16).
   - *You belong to me* (1 Peter 2:9).

# TEN

# DEEPLY CONNECTING
# WITH GOD

I've seen couples who seek premarital counseling, not necessarily as a way of preparing for their life journey together but because it is required by the pastors officiating their wedding ceremonies. Premarital couples tend to be more idealistic about their relationships than most married couples, and generally they do not have pressing relationship concerns. So when I am working with these couples, I usually begin the counseling process by gathering a history of their relationship. I am interested in what they can recall about how they met, what drew them to one another, and what led each of them to want to get married. Even more importantly, I make observations of their nonverbal cues to gauge their emotional connection in the relationship. I notice how they are positioned when sitting on the couch. I look for whether they exchange eye contact and initiate gestures of affection. I also listen to their tone of voice when talking about the relationship and each other.

Many couples think that if they don't have a lot of fights, their relationship is good and healthy. However, most relationship counselors know that the strength of the relationship is not the absence of conflicts but the strength of their emotional connection. When couples have a strong connection, it is much easier to resolve conflicts when they occur, and they can do so in a way that can even lead to deeper connection. For this reason, one of the key goals of premarital counseling is to help couples proactively work on strengthening their bond with each other.

Every human relationship requires effort to maintain our connection, and the same is true of our relationship with God. Proactive effort is required for us to feel connected to God and to experience him as a real presence in our lives. Our faith is more than a set of beliefs and practices; it is a relationship with the living God. As we learned in chapter 9, emotional connection is not created by simply wishing for it; we have to work at it and seek to create it.

When we really want something, it is in our nature to go after it whether it is good for us or not. The greatest barrier to emotional connection in any relationship is that we don't prioritize it until we actually feel the discomfort of disconnection or the hostility of conflict. The reason we have to work to maintain our connection with God goes back to our original design. Who we are and our worth are derived in relationship with him, so the stronger we feel connected with God, the deeper we will internalize who we are in him.

When we rest in God for our identity, the external crisis, no matter how devastating or frightening, can rage on because the core of our inner being will remain steady. We will be empowered to face whatever circumstances come our way.

In this chapter, we will examine the barriers that hinder our connection with God and consider ways in which we can proactively deepen our relationship with him.

## BARRIERS TO EMOTIONAL CONNECTION WITH GOD

When I realized what it meant to receive Christ into my heart, I immediately knew I had been given an identity that was unshakable. I was now a child of the King of the universe! Yet my conscious recognition of my identity in Christ did not instantaneously change how I related to him. In fact, I still struggle to feel like I am his child and trust in him to sovereignly rule over my life. And I'm certain I'm not alone in this. Based on the admission of many I've met in my office, the discrepancy between what we know about God in our minds and how we relate to him in our hearts is a common experience for at least two reasons. First, we have implicit beliefs about God that are operating unconsciously and are influenced by our lived experiences with our earthly parents or other significant figures in our lives. Second, our natural inclination toward self-redemption often relegates God, our beliefs, or our faith practices to being merely part of our idolatrous strategy to suppress our pain and assert an acceptable identity. Let's take a closer look at each of these barriers.

## RELATING TO GOD AS WE RELATED TO OTHERS

Experts who study attachment with God or our *God image* suggest that our view of God and how we relate to him corresponds to how we view and relate to significant figures in our early relationships.[1] The emotional/relational experiences in our early relationships with our caregivers form a template that becomes a way for us to make sense of other people as well as how we see and relate to God. This template works like a reflex and operates without our awareness. In my case, I saw my parents as loving but incapable of really helping me, especially in times of distress as a child. I experienced them as affectionate and warm, but they couldn't help me learn the language, do my homework, protect me from bullies, or help me manage my fears. So it was not hard for me to see God as a loving and warm figure, but not sovereign and capable to address all of my fears. Even though I knew in my head that God is all powerful, I didn't relate to him or rely on him as if this was true.

Instead, I believed that I had to work hard to take care of myself, that there are certain things that are my responsibility alone. I worked hard to find a job to provide for my family when my husband started his seminary training. I worked hard to try and figure out what we should do next after being let go from the church where we were serving. I worked hard to get pregnant when I was told that I would not be able to conceive without help. When I was distressed, my pattern was to jump into action, and God took the back seat. It's not that God was completely irrelevant in these situations. I prayed for his help to strengthen me and even guide me. But I could not find rest in him or really trust that he would provide without me working hard. I reached out to him but didn't experience peace. There was a disconnect. Because of my past experiences with my parents, I acted as if everything was all up to me, which led to the old painful feelings of being alone as I tried to handle things that felt overwhelming to me. As this pattern became more apparent, I realized that I did not know enough about who God really is to trust him. I related to him as if he did not have the power to change my circumstances or my distress without my own efforts to change them. I was relying on myself and disparaging his omnipotence in my life.

I still struggle with this today. However, being aware of this pattern motivates me to seek to know and understand aspects of God that are not fully real to me yet. When I got married at the age of twenty-four, I thought I knew the man I was marrying, having dated him for four years. Now, even after thirty-one years of marriage, I am often baffled by who he is and realize again and again there is much more to know about him. And this is the nature of relationships. As they deepen and grow in intimacy, we learn more about the other that we didn't know before. And if this is true of human relationships, how much more is it so with God? God is enormously vast, mysterious, and too magnificent for us to comprehend fully. There will always be something more to know about him.

If we are made to derive our identity from God, how we perceive God is crucial to knowing who we are and where our worth comes from. Our identity depends on who we believe is our *decisive validator*,[2] the one who gives us our identity. For example, if Emily's view of God is that he is critical and demanding like her earthly father, she will likely see herself as defective or not good enough in some way. Imagine if we really believed God is who he says he is in the Scriptures—all powerful, ever-present, all-knowing, sovereign, exalted above all other names, holy, and loving. How would his validation of who we are impact us? If we were to encounter his greatness and his majesty, we would be struck with awe, reverence, and admiration. And if this is the God who says we are his treasured possession (Deut. 7:6), that we are perfect and made holy (Heb. 10:10, 14), that we are chosen to be holy and blameless (Eph. 1:4), and that we are his children (Rom. 8:16), then imagine how these truths would shape our identity and worth. Hearing this affirmation from someone who not only knows us but holds supreme authority over all that exists will have immeasurable impact on how we see ourselves. Growing in our knowledge and understanding of *who God is* will enable us to realize our true identity, making it the core of who we are. Growing closer to God, we will see more of him. And as we see more of him, our sense of self and worth stabilizes.

To deepen our emotional connection with God, we need to recognize that our early relationships with significant figures in our lives can hinder us from knowing God as he is. But another barrier is our tendency to turn good things into ultimate things. Even in our relationship with God, our inclination for self-redemption manifests itself.

## IDOLATROUS STRATEGIES AND GOD

When I first learned how idolatry works—that good things can become ultimate things when we give them god-like importance and power—I realized how easily we can fall into idolatry. I noticed that I often depend on spiritual practices like prayer, devotions, church attendance, and serving others as a measure of my closeness to God or as a means to feel secure, as if I can avoid "bad" things happening to me by doing the right things. I noticed that the driver for my faith was often my sense of obligation and desire to be a "good" Christian, rather than my desire and affection for God himself. Moreover, I noticed how hard it is to actually discern my true motive for doing what I do. This is a common experience for many of us. I think this is why the Bible says, "The heart is deceitful above all things and beyond cure. Who can understand it?" (Jer. 17:9). Recognizing the tendencies of our hearts will help us to stay alert and mindful to avoid making something good, like our faith, into the ultimate thing. As we learned in chapter 5, our faith, spiritual practices, and even our notion of God can become part of our idolatrous strategies not only to suppress our pain but also to assert an identity that we deem worthy and good.

When we see God as he is and he becomes the center of our lives, our connection with him should directly affect our innate shame and ease the longing to be known and accepted. We may never be completely free from our shame or our longing for acceptance on this side of heaven, but as our relationship with God deepens, our reactions to our shame and longing can be better understood and can lead to deeper healing and growth. If our connection with God lacks depth, there is a danger that our faith and even God will be used as part of our idolatrous strategies for power, control, approval, and comfort.

For example, when we desire *power* too much we may seek positions of leadership or seek greater biblical knowledge for the purpose of influencing or dominating others in order to feel good about ourselves or feel that we are better than others. As this becomes a pattern, particularly for those in leadership positions, the inordinate desire for power can result in abuse of power, which can lead to massive damage to those serving under us as well as to the integrity of the Christian faith and its community.

When we desire *control* too much, we may perform our duties as believers or as rituals, going through the motions while our hearts aren't really engaged. We may attend church regularly, serve the church in various roles, and say and do all the "right" things. However, in our hearts, we are motivated to do these things to project an image of being spiritually mature or to gain a sense of security, like a formula to avoid what we fear and secure God's favor. This can be described as works-righteousness.

When we desire *approval* too much, we may engage in another form of works-righteousness. We do the right things and present ourselves in the right way to *get* God's affirmation and praise, rather than being motivated to do good because he has *already* saved and accepted us. We will seek to please him in order to be loved, rather than out of the overflow of grace he has given us. So even though we may do good or be good, we don't feel secure in who we are, making us overly sensitive to other people's reactions to us and judgments about us.

When we desire *comfort* too much, we may use God as an infinite source of forgiveness and comfort in our pain and sorrow, as well as an excuse to avoid responsibilities and protect ourselves from discomfort or potential harm. For example, we may refuse to work when we need employment, stating that God has called us to a certain profession, or we may avoid serving others or attending corporate worship, stating that we love God but not religious institutions.

Because our hearts are hard to understand, we need to ask God regularly to examine our hearts—"Search me, God, and know my heart. . . . See if there is any offensive way in me" (Ps. 139:23–24)—and listen to what the Holy Spirit reveals to us. The act of recognizing our heart's tendencies and thoroughly examining our hearts will keep us humble and more reliant on God to turn away from our idolatry before it sets in as a pattern of living life for us.

When we become aware of our barriers to connecting more deeply with God, we can do two things to begin to change our pattern: grieve and repent. First, when we recognize the correlation between how we view and relate to others and how we view and relate to God, we grieve the wounds of our past that block us from really knowing him. I've grieved that my parents could not protect me or assist me in my basic developmental needs such as acquiring the language. Emily will need to grieve that she did not have safe parents whom she could depend on. She can grieve not having a dad who made her feel loved and accepted and having a mom who was too bound by her own emotional pain to attune to Emily's fears and comfort her.

Second, as we become more aware of our self-reliance, we need to repent. Both Emily and I experienced an inordinate desire for control. We worked hard to suppress our pain and to feel worthy by overloading ourselves with responsibilities. Although we had different reasons, neither of us could rest and trust in God. I related to God as if he were incapable of helping me. Emily related to him as someone who was not safe but who expected her to get things right in order to be seen, accepted, and rewarded. We not only need to repent of our self-reliance but also of the way we perceive God and relate to him.

Being aware of and minimizing our *barriers* will help us feel closer to God, but we can also be more proactive about changing our ways of relating to him as we become more aware of our *patterns*.

## CREATING EMOTIONAL CONNECTION WITH GOD

To create an emotional connection with God means to have a personal encounter with God. God already knows us intimately, but when we come to realize his closeness to us, we experience an emotional connection. For example, in John 1:47–49, Nathanael was surprised by Jesus' recognition of who he was at their first meeting and asked, "How do you know me?" Jesus answered, "I saw you while you were still under the fig tree before Philip called you." His answer was ambiguous, perhaps even meaningless to us as readers, but Jesus' answer conveyed something so personal to Nathanael, he knew exactly what Jesus meant. Nathanael responded, "Rabbi, you are the Son of God; you are the king of Israel." It's not important for us to know what Nathanael was doing under the fig tree or what Jesus was referring to exactly. The point is that Nathanael realized who Jesus was because Jesus knew him in a personal way. The experience of feeling seen and known by God should cause us to see who God really is more clearly. And this is what we are after when we are connecting with him.

According to renowned relationship researcher John Gottman, deep, intimate connections between couples are created through hundreds of very ordinary, mundane moments in which they attempt to make emotional connections.[3] In my own marriage and in observing other couples, I've seen that those who have formed habits or rituals of mundane moments tend to feel closer to one another. Whether it's checking in with each other through a quick text or phone call during a workday, or praying or eating together at the end of each day, these habits become the context for creating and maintaining our emotional connections. Similarly, it's important for us to develop daily habits and rituals with God in which emotional connections can occur.

I first prayed the sinner's prayer as a six-year-old because I wanted to go to heaven and have all the bananas I could eat. That's what my Sunday school teacher said would happen if I accepted Christ into my heart. Later, as a thirteen-year-old, I was baptized. I was raised to believe that the spiritual discipline of having quiet time is an important component of being a Christian, and that if I wanted to grow in intimacy with God, I should set aside this time each day to spend one-on-one with God. I was taught to read and meditate on Scripture and pray as a daily habit. As I got older, and especially after getting married and having children, I began to realize how critical it is to habitually spend time with one another in order to stay connected. More than a required assignment, these dedicated times become occasions for extraordinary experiences of connection.

There are many good reasons for us to spend time with God. However, one of the most compelling is that we are made to derive our identity from God. This means it is imperative to know *who he is* in order to know *who we are.* I once heard in a sermon that being made in the image of God implies that we need to face the image we are to reflect and represent, like the moon reflects the sun. We cannot reflect and represent someone whom we do not know. So devoting regular times to spend with God to know him and experience being known by him is essential to our identity. Spending time with a body of believers, like worshiping with a congregation or participating in fellowship groups, Bible study groups, and corporate prayer meetings, and serving others, are also major building blocks to keeping our relationship with God from growing stagnant. But the focus of this chapter is about using our personal times with the Lord to deepen our connection with him.

To know God and to experience being known by him, it is necessary to spend time in his Word, which is his chosen way of revealing himself to us. However, what God reveals should also feel personal to us, as it did for Nathanael, and what we experience with God shouldn't just yield new insights about him but should evoke deeper affections for him. To build upon the foundational practice of having quiet times, I recommend adding the practice of visualizing his Word using the *imagination*, growing our affections for him through *worship*, and using our *senses* to experience God in more personal ways. When God says, "Love the Lord your God with all your heart and with all your soul and with all your strength and with all your mind" (Luke 10:27), we can respond by engaging our imagination, our emotions, and our human senses as well as our intellect.

## CONNECTING WITH GOD THROUGH OUR IMAGINATION

The first way to create an emotional connection with God is through using your imagination and visualizing the words on the pages of the Bible coming alive to interact with you. Because I relate to God as if he is incapable of helping me in times of distress, I often feel overwhelmed by what I perceive to be my responsibilities, which feel too big for me to handle alone. So when I imagine Jesus calming the storm, his power becomes more real to me than if I was just reading words on a page. I visualize the scene in my mind—the furious storm violently striking the boat, the disciples trying to stabilize it without success, their fear intensifying with each passing moment, and their bodies tensing up as they call out, "Don't you care, Jesus?" I've actually felt this way before and have said these exact words out loud to him. In the midst of this chaos, Jesus awakens and rebukes the wind and commands the waves to be still. Stillness and peace follow. In my mind, the scene unfolds, as real as any scene in a movie, and I am in awe of who he is.

As I engage my imagination to envision this story, I ask myself and the Lord what he might be showing me through this story. This summer was a particularly difficult season for me as I had to say goodbye to my dad who passed away after seven months of hospice care. I felt emotionally and physically depleted after having cared for him at my home while he was slowly dying. I witnessed the cruelty of the dying process, and after his passing I felt as if the life I'd known had changed drastically. The weight of losing the physical presence of my dad, who delighted in who I am, felt too much to bear. It seemed right for everything in the world to pause and give me time to reorient myself to a world where my dad no longer existed. But that didn't happen, of course. Nothing paused or even slowed down, and I had to move on and live life—shopping for groceries, preparing meals, seeing my clients, having meetings, and writing this book.

Although I was not in a boat in the middle of a raging storm, I felt overwhelmed. The voice of fear was activated inside of me. *This is too much! You're never going to make it!* In the middle of storms like this within me, Jesus appears to gently rebuke my fears, to tell me to relax and be still. I can hear him saying to me, *It's okay. I know you're afraid, but I am here with you. You do what you can—that's all that's required.* Visualizing the story of Jesus calming the storm made his power more real to me. I saw and understood that he is more powerful than what I am afraid of.

Seeing him as who he is helps me to feel calm because I know he is able to handle whatever overwhelms me. Unlike my experiences as a child, I can trust the one who is in the "boat" with me. I can trust God to take care of me and the concerns that threaten me. He calms the storm inside of me. He directly addresses my distress. This story from the Bible has become personal to me. I have felt Jesus' closeness and been in awe of who he is.

## GROWING OUR AFFECTIONS FOR GOD THROUGH WORSHIP

More often than not, I run to God when I am in tough situations or feeling distressed. However, I've learned that what helps us face adversity with peace—even more than asking God to help us through our requests—is *seeing who he really is*. When we see God for who he is, adoration and worship will naturally flow out of us, just as I shared in the example above. But because I am wired to simply run to God when I need his help, I know I must make a conscious effort to get myself to reflect on who he really is. I have found that worshiping God through music or songs can be another effective way to grow my affections for him.

It has been said that music is the language of the soul. It certainly has been an integral part of the human experience for as long as humanity has been around. In fact, the Johns Hopkins Center for Music and Medicine has been conducting studies to learn how music affects the brain and the body's systems, and they have found that music activates a host of different areas of the brain. Some of these studies suggest that making music stimulates more parts of the brain than any other human activity and can even change the structure of our brains by creating new neural pathways and rewiring parts of our brain networks.[4] I find this interesting because our God image (or how we relate to God) requires changes in our brain as well. New relational/emotional experiences can revise our God image, and music may be another way to facilitate that change.

We have all experienced the power of music. It helps us to relax. It gives us goose bumps. It evokes emotions in us, moving us to tears, exhilaration, and joy. When our adoration and affections for God are aroused, we not only feel close to him, but the experience revises our God image. Consider the lyrics and tune of your favorite hymn or praise song. What feelings does it evoke? What does it cause you to feel about God? Perhaps reflect on the familiar words of the famous hymn "How Great Thou Art."

When I sing this hymn, my gaze turns away from my fears and my worries. I am able to see who God is in my present world. When we sing songs of praise, we feel reverence for God but also a sense of fondness and admiration. Relationship researchers say that healthy, emotionally connected couples feel a fondness for each other and admire qualities in each other. Fondness and admiration involves more than knowing the other; it involves affection and emotions for the other. Worship through music and song not only helps us experience fondness and admiration for our God but also rewires our brains, integrating the left and right brain to change *how* we relate to him.

## USING OUR PHYSICAL SENSES TO CONNECT WITH GOD

It's one thing to know in our minds that God is with us, but it's another to sense his presence. What I've shared in this section—visualization and worship through songs—involves our senses. When we visualize, we are using our imagination, and when our emotions are evoked through worship, we can sense our bodies loosening up. A sense of calmness sets in as we sing songs acknowledging who God is and expressing our affections for him.

But these are just the tip of the iceberg. There are many additional ways we can experience connection with God. With today's scientific advancements, we are observing more evidence of the interconnectedness between the body and the soul. Since we are spiritual beings with physical bodies, God regularly uses the capacities of our bodies to create connection with him.

In the movie *Chariots of Fire*, the missionary and Olympic runner Eric Liddell famously says, "God made me fast, and when I run I feel his pleasure."[5] Running fast made Liddell feel closer to God. Others of us may have different ways in which we experience closeness with God, but quite often they involve some form of physical experience. For example, some have shared with me that sitting quietly in the pew of a sanctuary makes them feel close to God. Others have said that gazing into the horizon as the sun rises and sets or looking up at the night sky makes them feel close to God. We all have special places and objects that stir up fond memories and feelings for the people we love, and similarly we can have special places we go or objects we carry with us that help us feel connected to God and sense his presence with us.

Two weeks ago, I attended a memorial service for a dear friend and mentor whom I loved. After the celebration of her life and spending time with others who also loved her, I felt an emptiness set in within me that I cannot adequately describe in words. The service was held near a beach I had often visited with my dad, as well as on my own. I feel close to God when I am on a beach, listening to the sound of waves, looking out at the vastness of the ocean, and breathing in the ocean breeze as I am reminded of God's great power and majesty. So I decided to stop by the beach that day to spend some time with the Lord—no words, just tears. After some time crying, I noticed that the drizzle of rain had lightened and the sun was peeking through the clouds. As my eyes shifted from the ocean to the sky, there appeared the most beautiful rainbow I have ever seen. I couldn't help but say out loud, "Wow!" My tears of emptiness turned to tears of comfort and joy. It felt like God had a personal message for me: *I see you. I am here with you. Let me give you a hug.* I felt comforted and assured that God saw my broken heart. He let me know that I wasn't alone. When it really sinks in who God is and that he loves me and is with me, I am blown away—and my heart's response is some version of "How Great Thou Art!"

Have you ever experienced being with someone whose presence alone made your tense shoulders relax, settled the butterflies in your stomach, and made you breathe better, feeling calm and at peace? You don't have to say anything, but you feel seen and you know that this person understands what you are going through and how you are feeling, and is feeling it with you. You feel at ease, even if nothing is resolved, because just being together grounds you. I've had few such experiences in my lifetime, but this is what I hope to achieve in my relationship with God.

In every relationship, the most important thing we can do to deepen our connection with one another is to learn continuously about the other. This is true with God as well. Keep seeking him to know him. And when we have these experiences of closeness with him, it is critical to put our experiences into words and share them with others as a way of solidifying the experiences. When we put words to our experiences, they become more real and memorable for us. Never forget that the depth of your connection with God has huge implications for your identity. Because when you know who God actually is, you will know who you are, and your identity will be stable and secure through the storms of life.

# *Reflection*

God made us to have a relationship with him. Consider what it would look like for you to strengthen your bond with God.

1. When do you feel closest to God? Is it when going to a special place, meditating on his Word, praying, singing, or some other experience?
2. Identify a specific Bible passage or a song or hymn that is meaningful to you. What feelings come up for you as you read the passage or sing the song?
3. Tell God about how you feel in prayer, or write a letter to God about your feelings toward him.
4. Share about your experience with God with someone you trust.

CONCLUSION

# BEING WHO YOU ARE
# CREATED TO BE

In our culture today, our preoccupation with defining our own identity is hard to ignore. In fact, this has been a recurring theme in the history of human existence. The preoccupation with the self, whether it manifests in self-enhancement strategies or biases, is often considered simply part of being human. However, when we look at this pre-occupation with the self through a biblical lens, we know that something went very wrong with our human nature when sin separated us from God our Creator. The ultimate end to our perpetual search for who we are is only possible when we are able to reconnect with God. God's rescue plan for a lost humanity is the gospel, which sets us free from the verdict of sin and justifies us as his prized possession. When we internalize this gospel, his message of love, we come to know who we are more and more, stabilizing our core identity as God's children.

I imagine there are many more things that I do not know about people than I do know about them. However, I know for certain that we were made to be in relationship with God, to understand who we are and our worth in him. Although the problem of our identity is ultimately a spiritual one, our experience is complicated by living in a physical body in a fallen world. We are born with internalized shame that is reinforced and personalized through our experiences of pain. Moreover, our reliance on ourselves to fix our shame-based identity gets us stuck in a perpetual cycle of striving.

The good news of the gospel, however, can set us free from our striving, because when Christ gave his life to atone for our sins and reconciled us to God, he reconnected us to the source of our identity. This does not mean that every other aspect of our identity is irrelevant. But our identity in him is the primary, grounding foundation of who we are that helps us to order all of the other aspects of our identity that make us each unique. To the degree we are able to receive healing for our wounds and relinquish our idolatrous strategies, we will be more able to deeply internalize the gospel. And the more we deeply internalize the gospel, the more we will be free from our past pain and our strategies that entangle us.

The process of internalizing the gospel is a gradual process that includes unearthing wounds of our past that still affect us in our present life as well as grieving our pain. It requires us to be mindful of how easily our strategies can become idolatrous as a way to suppress our pain and the attempt to achieve an acceptable identity on our own, so that we can repent of our reliance on them rather than depending on Christ's finished work on the cross. As we grow in our awareness of how sin has impacted us—specifically, the pain of our shame and core hurts as well as our idolatrous strategies—we can grieve and repent over hiding our brokenness and striving for an identity of our own making.

To internalize the gospel is to deepen our relationship with God. They are one and the same. What we know about God should become a lived experience for us, in which God is not just a belief but a person. And just like any human relationship, our relationship with God requires intentionality to strengthen our connection and intimacy with him. We need to remind ourselves again and again of who he is and who we are in him, and to experience how high, wide, and vast his love is for us. At times we may grow complacent and think we already know that God loves us. But people need reminders that they are loved, valued, and appreciated. It's not enough to get married and expect that because you made those vows, your spouse will never need reminded of your love. Nor can you simply provide materially for a child and expect that child will know your affections for him or her. Relationships require relational engagement. Remember, there is a longing within us to be known and accepted, and while this longing is exacerbated by our shame, as it is met with God's love and acceptance, our shame loosens its grip on who we are. So it's not enough to just know God loves us; we need to experience his love. Throughout this book, I've sought to describe a way of examining ourselves to remove the barriers to deepen our connection with him, based on my research and counseling experience. We will also need a community of believers to help us see where we are broken and to receive tangible experiences of God's love and acceptance. And we'll need to use all of our human senses—exercising our imaginations, evoking emotions and sensations through music, naming sacred spaces or rituals that hold personal meaning for us—to more fully experience God's matchless love in personal ways.

As our relationship with God deepens, our preoccupation with ourselves will lessen. In fact, we will begin to experience greater self-acceptance, knowing we are broken and yet dearly loved. This shift in our identities will not only help us better regulate our emotions and alleviate symptoms such as anxiety or depression, but it will also change the way we make sense of our experiences, giving us new purpose and hope for our lives even in our suffering. Furthermore, it will change the way we view and relate to other people. Having experienced grace in relationship with God, we will be better able to extend forgiveness to others and be more accepting of others' shortcomings. We will also be able to establish communities for mutual support and growth in our relationship with God.

We are certain to face struggles and heartaches living as broken people in an imperfect world. Deriving our identity from God will not necessarily spare us from suffering and pain, but it will shift our interpretation of what we experience and enable us, by the power of the indwelling Spirit, to remain steady for the long journey, knowing who we are and our worth in Christ.

As you finish this book and consider your next steps, I encourage you to be curious and explore your life stories. Are there events or experiences that you would like to forget, perhaps that you've never talked about? How did you survive these difficult experiences, and have you considered how God fits in with them? What strategies do you use to cover up your pain and give yourself an identity? Are you feeling stuck, without much hope of breaking free from certain fears, patterns, or sins? Are there people in your life that you can process these questions with? An exercise is included in appendix A for you to use when you are feeling triggered or reacting in a way that you don't fully understand.

When shame is met with grace, it loses its power to define who we are. I encourage you to seek counseling to deepen your healing and strengthen your identity in Christ as you explore the answers to these questions and find your buried treasures. He will rescue us from ourselves and set us free from our striving to resolve our shame. So let us fix our eyes on Jesus, the author and perfecter of our faith, who for the joy set before him endured the cross, scorning its shame, and sat down at the right hand of the throne of God. Let us consider him who endured such opposition from sinners, so that we will not grow weary and lose heart (Heb. 12:2–3).

# ACKNOWLEDGMENTS

I give thanks to God, my Redeemer, for his constant assurance of his presence with me throughout the process of writing this book. He is the author of my story, and I am grateful for the many experiences that have brought me closer to knowing who I am in him. So I give God all praise and glory for the completion of this book!

This book represents the collective wisdom of many counselors at Redeemer Counseling gained through experience and research. I especially want to acknowledge Peter Cha and Lois Kehlenbrink, who started the journey with me more than twenty years ago, and Olimpio Wen and Ellen Lee, who later joined our efforts as the main contributors in developing the Gospel-Centered Integrative Framework for Therapy (GIFT). I have learned enormously from their biblical insights and clinical expertise, but more than that, I have been constantly moved by their heart for God and his truth to be the center of our work. The GIFT would not have been possible without their heart and labor. I want to acknowledge the clinical supervisors at Redeemer

Counseling—Natasha Steenkamp, Raymond Corbo, Linda Foran, Kate Glerup, Jyothi James, Sharon Richards, Hilary Chiu, Rebecca Beidel, Christina Choi, Rosalin Brueck, and Susannah Atkins—for applying the GIFT in their work, expanding and clarifying how the GIFT can be applied more effectively, and training our staff in using the GIFT. I want to acknowledge Dr. Elena Kim, a psychologist and researcher, who designed and conducted research to help us analyze the GIFT and identified key steps in how we can help people internalize the gospel. We share the same desire for the gospel to be relevant in psychotherapy.

I want to acknowledge Kathy Keller for reading our developmental papers on GIFT and giving us invaluable insights to strengthen our understanding of gospel-centered counseling care. Of course I want to acknowledge Timothy Keller for significantly shaping me in how I think about people and how to help them through counseling but, most importantly, for helping me experience God's grace and deepening my relationship with God. To read more about Tim and Kathy's influence on me, please refer to my essay "Counseling: Tearing Down the Idols," in *The City for God: Essays Honoring the Work of Timothy Keller* (Square Halo Books, 2022).

Finally, I want to acknowledge the many clients who have sought counseling at Redeemer Counseling, especially those who have participated in our studies. I have learned tremendously through their courageous endeavors to heal and grow, and I continue to be inspired by them to become better as a counselor and a follower of Christ.

Much of the content in this book is my synthesis of what

I've learned from Tim and Kathy Keller, my esteemed colleagues, my clients, and my research.

The process of putting this book together also required the gifts and labor of many special people. I want to thank Kathleen Hahn for managing this project, working with our agent, attorney, and publisher to handle all the logistics, and for her constant effort to protect my boundaries to keep me sane throughout the writing process. Thanks go to my team of readers—Josue Calderon, Alyssa Plock, and Kathleen Hahn—for reading my many drafts and for honest feedback to set me on the path to reach the readers. I want to thank Clara Kim, my collaborative writer, for believing in this project from the beginning and introducing me to a wonderful agent, Don Gates, who also believed in the potential for this book. If it wasn't for Clara's enthusiasm and willingness to partner with me throughout this process, I would not have started on this journey. I am also grateful for her incredible knack for words to make my technical writing more readable and accessible. And thanks to the RCS team. I would not have had the courage and strength to finish this book without the support and prayers of my team!

Now, I want to thank the special people in my life who have shaped who I am today. Thanks to Paul Tripp, my first supervisor at Redeemer Counseling, for anchoring me on my career path. His encouragement to run toward my fears gave me the courage to remain as a counselor back in 1998. Thanks to Andi and Lourine, my spiritual mentors, for being there for me in my times of distress, guiding me in my growth, and modeling God's tender love for me. Thanks to my dear friends Jobey and Jenny for teaching me to celebrate God's beauty in me and for their prayers. And thanks to my family who have been my steady source of encouragement and support throughout my life. I am grateful for their patience with me when I was too distracted to be present and for the many "You can do it" encouragements to keep me going throughout the writing process. I want to thank my husband, Peter, for teaching me what it means to love and for the countless conversations we've had about counseling. I've learned the most from him about what it looks like to have people experience God through what we do. Thank you to my precious daughters, Karis and Elise, for their tech support and for being my sounding board for what I want to communicate in this book. Just by being in my life, they've inspired me to live out the contents of this book. Thanks to my sister, Susan, and brother, Steve, for their companionship throughout my life, especially our early years in America. The hard times were much more bearable because they were with me in them. My story has been richly blessed by their presence in my life.

# A PERSONAL EXERCISE: WHAT ARE MY FEELINGS TRYING TO TELL ME?

**H**ave you noticed what you are feeling lately? Perhaps you've been curt and irritable with your loved ones, struggled for weeks to get a good night's sleep, or burst into tears at the most unexpected times and wondered, *What's wrong with me?* If you've been perplexed by your reactions, you are not alone.

In counseling we want people to know that when they don't make sense of their emotions, they will continue to react to them automatically, thus remaining stuck in a reactive cycle that can bring more harm to themselves and others. We also want them to know that experiencing these feelings is not sinful or a sign of weakness. In fact, being curious and processing these feelings can reveal the heart's desires that have become idolatrous and the deeper wounds that need God's healing.

We all have desires, but they can become too important, elevating good things to ultimate things as a way to avoid our pain and feel okay about ourselves. Just as we are often not fully aware of the impact of painful experiences in our past, we are also unaware when these desires evolve and become demands—not just what we want, but what we must have or do. This is why when we actually notice and follow our feelings, we are getting closer to answering the question "What's wrong with me?"

So, with attentiveness and intentionality, we invite you to explore what is going on behind your feelings by following these steps:

## STEP 1: EXPLORE "WHAT'S THE DESIRE BEHIND HOW I FEEL?"

1. Recognize the feeling you are experiencing. (We will use the feelings of annoyance, frustration, or anger, but fill in your feelings as you recognize them.)
2. Recall the last time you felt annoyed, frustrated, or angry, and allow yourself to feel the feeling by verbalizing or writing down the circumstance in which you experienced this feeling.
3. As you recall, notice whether you are judging or being critical of your feelings, and tell the judging/critical part of you that everything is okay and that you want to hear what those feelings are saying.
4. Behind the feeling, there is an unmet desire. Often these desires show up as "should" statements:

    a. I should be able to . . .
    b. I should be treated . . .
    c. I should have . . .
    d. I should be . . .
5. Identify your desires. Remember that your desires are more than likely valid, but your feelings of annoyance, frustration, or anger may indicate that your desires have become too important/idolatrous.

## STEP 2: EXPLORE "WHAT ARE THE 'I AM . . .' MESSAGES BEHIND MY DESIRES?"

1. Refrain from condemning yourself for your idolatrous desires, but understand that your heart's desires became idolatrous in an effort to avoid the pain of your wounds. You can acknowledge the idolatrous desire, but also empathize with why it has become so important to you.
2. Remain curious and reflect on what is behind your desires. When our desires are unmet, we inevitably make interpretations that convey something about ourselves to make sense of why we don't have what we should. These interpretations of ourselves reinforce the sense that something is wrong with us.
3. Recall a significantly difficult or painful memory in your life story and identify the messages you got about yourself in that experience. These messages are shame-based and often say either:
    a. I am . . . (worthless, unlovable, etc.)
    b. I am not . . . (good enough, important, etc.)

## STEP 3: MAKE THE CONNECTION BETWEEN YOUR IDOLATROUS DESIRES AND YOUR INTERNALIZED BELIEFS ABOUT YOURSELF

For example, if your desire is to be married, then not being married may reinforce the message that you are not good enough. The feelings of frustration or anger will make better sense when you understand what desires and beliefs reside in your heart.

When you know what is behind your feelings, your interaction with God will also change. Rather than just asking for God's help with your feelings or asking for forgiveness for your reactions, you can honestly express your heart to God and receive his affirmation for the root cause of your reactions.

Note that processing emotions is often helpful when it is done with another person whom you trust and with whom you feel safe. If you've felt numb for some time or have trouble accessing your feelings, it may be best to seek a trained professional to help guide the process.

## STEP 4: EXPRESS WHAT IS GOING ON INSIDE OF YOU TO GOD

When you are engaging with God directly, imagine you are in his presence, talking with him, and allow for honest emotional disclosure.

1. Tell God your feelings of annoyance, frustration, and anger.
2. Tell God you feel this way because you long for your desires to be fulfilled.

3. Tell God how you had hoped that getting what you desire would resolve your pain.
4. Admit that your way of resolving the "I am" message isn't working.
5. Ask God for his forgiveness and to help you believe that Christ has already resolved your shame.

Lastly, listen for God's response to you and respond to him. Often our desires are not something we need to relinquish, but rather to grieve that they have evolved and affected who we are.

## APPENDIX B

# FOR PASTORS AND CAREGIVERS: HOW DO I KNOW IF SOMEONE NEEDS COUNSELING?

The answer to the question "How do I know if someone needs counseling?" in part depends on how we define the purposes of counseling and what counseling is all about.

In a broader sense, those who are curious about themselves and are interested in exploring their inner world in order to grow can benefit greatly from counseling. Since the ultimate purpose for counseling from a Christian perspective is not merely symptom relief, but whole-person transformation, and since we all are broken people living in a broken world, anyone can benefit from the experience of counseling.

At the same time, counseling is certainly designed to help people who are experiencing distress and whose coping strategies have been ineffective. Oftentimes before people can delve deeper into root issues, they need to address any symptoms that are interfering with their daily functioning. Since pastoral and lay counselors help people with varying degrees of symptoms and distress, they often seek wisdom for knowing when to refer people to counseling professionals.

Both professional and lay counseling involve a relationship between the person in need of care and the care provider. Therefore, the discernment to know when to refer depends on the person's care needs and your capacity to care for those needs.

For anyone in the role of providing pastoral care, whether you are a pastor, ministry staff, or a small group leader, it is important to keep this question in mind, because not everyone God sends your way is someone whom you must care for, at least not alone. Sometimes it is clear when someone needs counseling, but at other times, it is harder to know. In either case, it is helpful to have professional counselors in your area to whom you can refer people or with whom you can consult when you are unsure about someone's care needs.

Some situations are fairly clear. When the person in need discloses that they are struggling with significant trauma, such as abuse, sexual assault, domestic violence, or severe symptoms like panic attacks, suicidal thoughts, or addictive behaviors, professional counseling care will be more appropriate for their needs.

Now, let's consider situations in which you are not certain if you should make a referral or not.

## ASSESSING THE CARE NEED OF THE PERSON

When assessing a person's need, we must gather their subjective experience of symptoms and how much these symptoms are interfering with their daily life. Below are four key areas for assessment:

1. **EXPLORE HOW INTENSELY THE PERSON IS FEELING THEIR SYMPTOMS.** As the person describes their circumstances, you may identify symptoms that require further examination.

   a. **PHYSIOLOGICAL SYMPTOMS:** These are behavioral reactions that are observable, such as sleeping or eating patterns or self-harming behaviors or addictions. For example, you can ask:

   - "How are you sleeping/eating?" If the person is sleeping less than four hours per night, or is hardly eating or binge eating, this would indicate a high intensity of symptoms.

   - "How often do you drink, and how much do you drink? On a scale of 1 to 10 (1 is strong ability and 10 is no ability), how would you rate your ability to control your urges to drink?" If the person is drinking almost every day, getting intoxicated, and indicates above 5 on the scale, this indicates that something more than pastoral care is needed.

b. **PSYCHOLOGICAL SYMPTOMS:** These are internal processes, such as thoughts and emotions, that are distressing. Scaling questions are helpful in assessing the person's subjective experience. For example, you can ask:

- "When you say that your mind is racing, on a scale of 1 to 10 (1 being least intense and 10 being most intense), where would you say you are?"
- "When you say you are feeling overwhelmed, on a scale of 1 to 10, where would you say you are?"
- A score of 7 or higher would indicate that something more than pastoral care is needed.

2. **EXPLORE HOW LONG THE PERSON HAS EXPERIENCED THEIR SYMPTOMS.** In addition to knowing how intense their symptoms are, it is important to know when they first experienced those symptoms. In general, the longer they have experienced the symptoms, the more likely it is that they would need to seek counseling care. You can ask the following questions:

- "When did you first experience these changes/symptoms?"
- "How long have you been struggling with your drinking?"
- "Do you feel like your struggles have gotten worse over time?"

If you've assessed that the person has mild to moderate symptoms, but they have experienced these symptoms for a period of three months or more, it would be best to involve a professional counselor in their care.

3. **EXPLORE WHETHER THE PERSON HAS EXPERI-ENCED THESE SYMPTOMS BEFORE.** If the person has experienced these symptoms before, it may be an indication that the problem is more serious. In that case, it will also be helpful to know how the person addressed these symptoms in the past. You can ask the following questions:
   - "Have you experienced these symptoms before, or have you struggled like this before?"
   - "Have you sought help for this before?"

   If the person indicates that they have struggled in the past and have sought help before, then it may be wise to seek professional care again.

4. **EXPLORE WHETHER THE PERSON IS ABLE TO FULFILL THEIR RESPONSIBILITIES.** High levels of distress affect the person's capacity to function as usual. Their usual responsibilities, such as going to work or caring for themselves or their children, can become too difficult to manage. For example, a person who has struggled with anxiety reports he is not able to leave his apartment to go to work or to get groceries. The more they are unable to fulfill their responsibilities, the more serious their care need. You can ask:
   - "Are you able to go to work or school or to care for your children?"
   - "Are you taking care of yourself?" The ability to care for the self ranges from personal hygiene to buying their food.

If the person answers no to any of these questions, it will be best to involve a professional counselor. If the person's ability to function is at a moderate level, you should follow up to see if they are improving. If the level of functioning remains unchanged or gets worse, then involve a professional counselor.

Even after you have assessed the person's need and determined they may not require professional counseling care, it is still important for you to assess your own capacity as a caregiver.

## ASSESS YOUR CAPACITY AS A CAREGIVER

Once you have a good sense of the care needed, you can assess what you can offer as the care provider. Your ability to provide effective care is dependent on the following:

1. **YOUR SKILLS.** Are you equipped with the knowledge and skills necessary to provide adequate care?
2. **YOUR AVAILABILITY.** Can you devote the time needed to provide adequate care for the person in need?
3. **YOUR CAPACITY.** Do you have the emotional and psychological bandwidth to share in the person's concerns? It is important to reflect on your capacity to ensure that you do not become overwhelmed and compromise your own well-being. This is particularly true if you have not worked through your own hurts and habits, since you may be triggered in the process of helping the person in need.

This assessment process will help determine if you are the caregiver for the person in need. As the diagram below shows, the greater the severity, the higher the required level of skills, availability, and capacity.

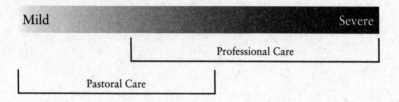

If more formal counseling care is needed:

- Your responsibility is then to make a referral and engage with the person until the transition of care is complete.
- Once the transition is complete, you can decide if you would like to remain involved in the care process. You can do that by actively collaborating with the counselor or by simply maintaining a supportive role by checking in regularly with the person in need and encouraging continued care.

# APPENDIX C

# HOW TO FIND A COUNSELOR WHO IS A GOOD MATCH FOR ME

**W**hen we seek counseling, we are engaging in a relationship with the person who is counseling us. In every interaction we have with people, there is potential for change, especially in the way we see ourselves and others. So counseling is primarily *a relationship* in which we hope to feel safe enough to reveal the broken parts of ourselves, explore our past, and identify the ways we have developed to deal with our pain and counter our shame. It is also a relationship in which we can have corrective relational experiences that revise our implicit beliefs about God.

Similar to any relationship, it is hard to discern if a counselor is a good fit for us until we are actually engaged in the relationship. At the same time, we can do our due diligence and be selective about who we entrust to partner with us on our journey toward change, healing, and growth. Here are a few guidelines to consider in your search:

1. **KNOW THE RANGE OF CHRISTIAN COUNSELING AVAILABLE.** Modern psychology was developed (largely atheistically) by doctors and scientists who were following a scientific method. Christian counselors have responded to the findings of modern psychology in different ways.

Some choose to embrace the findings of psychology, perhaps receiving their training at an entirely secular institution, and perhaps not explicitly using the Bible or prayer at all unless their clients actually bring matters of faith into the counseling process. So they may or may not integrate theology in their practice of counseling, but we should not assume they are any less godly or able to model Christ to their clients.

Others practice counseling in a much more explicitly Christian context, such as a church or Christian institution, or receive their training at a seminary. Of course, they can more explicitly discuss matters of faith, Scripture, and prayer in the counseling process. Counselors who identify as *biblical counselors* or *pastoral counselors* are usually informed about psychological concepts and practices but mainly base their counseling process on theology and the Bible.

From my perspective, having been trained in both biblical counseling and secular psychology, these views are not always incompatible with each other, and we have much to learn from both. Regardless, Christian counseling will vary in range of integration between theology and psychology depending on the context of practice. Oftentimes getting a referral from others you trust, such as from those in churches, seminaries, or who are trusted friends can help narrow your search.

2. **KNOW YOUR NEED.** To find a good fit, it is also important to know your level of need. In general, if you answer yes to any of the following questions, you may want to see a counselor with more experience with your particular concern.

   - *Have you been struggling with your present need not just recently but over a period of years?*
   - *Are there changes in the level of your functioning? Are you having trouble caring for yourself, going to school or work, socializing, or taking care of your responsibilities?*
   - *Have you been diagnosed with a mental health disorder?*
   - *Are you taking medication prescribed by a psychiatrist?* When you are under the care of multiple care providers, such as a doctor or psychiatrist, it is important that all your care providers are open to collaborating with one another.
   - *Are you lacking a supportive social network (family, friends, church life, and so on)?* Receiving counseling is not a magic bullet to fix all of your problems. Because deep change does not happen in isolation, it is important that your circle of social support goes beyond the counseling relationship. If

you are lacking this, then one of your counseling goals should be to expand this circle of support.

3. **KNOW THE COUNSELOR'S CREDENTIALS.** Counselors often have websites to introduce their services that include their qualifications and experience. If not, they should provide an informed consent, which includes the description of treatment they can provide. Some counselors in private practice may offer an initial ten- to fifteen-minute consultation for you to at least meet them and ask questions. Here are a few questions that may be helpful in determining fit:

- *How long have you been in practice?* The greater your need, the likelier you are to want to see counselors with more experience.
- *Are you licensed to practice?* Having a license does not indicate whether the counselor is good at what they do, but it does add accountability to a licensing board that requires them to adhere to the standards of their profession. If you are hoping to get reimbursed through insurance for your counseling care, most insurance plans require a licensed professional as the provider.
- *What training or experience have you obtained in the area I am seeking counseling for?* Often specializations are connected to additional training/ experience. Asking this question should not be offensive to a counselor.
- *How do you address the issue of faith and God in the therapy context?* This question may help you

to gauge how the counselor integrates theology and psychology.

- *When you work with clients who have multiple care providers, how do you work with them?* If you have other care providers, such as a psychiatrist or other doctors related to your mental health, it is important to find someone willing to collaborate with your other care providers for the most comprehensive care.

4. **AS YOU ENGAGE, CONTINUE TO ASSESS FOR FIT.** There is a limit to how much you can know about a counselor before you actually engage in the counseling process. So assessing whether you have a good fit is a continuous process. Here are a few questions to help guide you:

- *Do you feel at ease with your counselor? Are you able to share more deeply without feeling afraid of your counselor's judgment?* It is important that you feel safe to reveal more about yourself. If you are feeling increasingly uncomfortable, you should let your counselor know. The process of exploring your discomfort may lead to resolving it. Or, if your counselor gets emotional, defensive, or withdraws because of your feedback, it may not be a healthy counseling situation to remain in.
- *Does the counselor ask good questions in ways that help you go deeper in your process?* Counselors should have the skill to help you learn more about yourself.

- *Are your symptoms improving, and are you better able to fulfill your responsibilities?* You are seeking care in order to feel better and function better. You should experience a gradual shift in how you feel, think, and behave.

- *Are you making connections between your past and present? Are you discovering more about yourself?* Your wounds and idolatrous strategies from your past still play out in the present. To heal from your past wounds and to be freed from your strategies, you have to explore your past and see how it is affecting you today. Understanding your story from past to present will help you shape your future story.

- *Are you able to talk with your counselor about God in meaningful ways? Do you experience Christlikeness in your counselor?* For counseling to address all aspects of you, God has to be relevant in the counseling process. Talking about God with your counselor, as well as the counselor modeling Christ to you in how they approach you, will help you deepen your understanding of God.

- *Do you feel like you are getting closer to God?* As you become more aware of who you are, you should also grow in knowledge of God and experience more closeness to him.

As Christians, we know that the ultimate source of healing and change is God, and the ultimate goal of Christian counseling is to help us draw closer to him. However, depending on where we are on our journey, we have to prioritize the care we seek. For example, if we are experiencing panic attacks, meditating on God's Word or praying to deepen connection with God may not help us immediately. We may need medication or somatic interventions to alleviate the panic attack and stabilize our symptoms as well as meditating and praying. So, discerning what we need in the present will help narrow our options for counselors.

Since our relationship with a counselor is a professional one, the relationship is not a permanent one. Counselors are people who journey with us for a season. We can pause and return to counseling as concerns arise or as we identify the next area of healing/ growth or encounter various experiences in life, and we can also find another counselor who is more appropriate for that season in life to accompany us.

# GLOSSARY

*Adverse childhood experiences (ACEs)* are experiences of childhood trauma and adversity, such as abuse, neglect, poverty, and witnessing violence in the home or community, which lead to prolonged or excessive activation of the stress response system.

*Core hurts* are our repeated experiences of pain and suffering that reinforce our shame and personalize shame messages about ourselves.

*Corrective relational experiences* are experiences of feeling seen, heard, and understood in a relationship, which are new relational/emotional experiences that contradict our unconscious beliefs about ourselves, others, and God. As these new relational experiences are repeated over and over again, our beliefs about ourselves, others, and God also shift.

*Deep idols* are the inordinate desires for power, control, approval, and comfort that turn good things into ultimate things. These are the motivations/desires that rule our hearts, which are part of our idolatrous strategies.

*Explicit memory* is one form of long-term memory that we can bring to our conscious awareness when we are attentive and intentional.

*God concepts* are the intellectual or theological understandings we have of God; also referred to as head knowledge of God.

*God images*, which are stored in our implicit memory, are the ways a person emotionally or relationally experiences God; also known as heart knowledge of God.

*Gospel-Centered Integrative Framework for Therapy (GIFT)* is a framework for counseling developed at Redeemer Counseling, which provides a theoretical framework for the integration of theology and psychology as well as clinical structures for defining the underlying problem. It also provides guidelines for treatment to best help people experience the gospel and lasting heart change.

*Grieving and accepting* is a process in counseling to help people identify past wounds to express the full range of emotions associated with their pain and accept what is broken in them in order to help them more deeply internalize the gospel.

*Idolatrous strategies* are the strategies within the system of self-redemption. These are the particular self-reliant ways we deal with our shame and core hurts. We proactively utilize idolatrous strategies to assert an acceptable identity, hide parts of us, and satisfy our desires for power, control, approval, and comfort.

*Implicit memory* is one of the two main types of long-term memory. It is acquired and used unconsciously and affects our thoughts, feelings, and behaviors. Our templates for interpretation formed in our past wounds are stored in our implicit memory.

*Implicit relational representations (IRR)* are unconscious mental representations of the self, others, and God formed from experiences in early relationships with caregivers. These serve as templates to make relational interpretations and shape our subsequent behaviors.

*Internalized shame* is the unconscious sense in all humanity that something is wrong with us, which is the result of sin and is the basis for defining our view of self.

*Reactive emotions* are the emotions we feel when our idolatrous strategies fail and our core hurts are triggered, reinforcing our internalized shame.

*Surface idols* are any tangible objects, persons, or pursuits that become too important in our lives, such as money, career, sex, or children. Our deep idols are the *underlying* motivation that fuels our pursuit of good things, evolving them into ultimate things (surface idols).

*System of self-redemption (SOSR)* is an internal system that develops as a result of our alienation from God and our brokenness in a fallen world. It is a complex system of the heart formed in the context of our personal narratives that we develop in order to redeem our broken view of self and validate our identity, purpose, and worth apart from God. SOSR is a comprehensive lens of defining the problem in the GIFT.

# ABOUT REDEEMER
# COUNSELING

Redeemer Counseling is the largest Christian counseling center in New York City. The center began as an extension of pastoral care at Redeemer Presbyterian Church in 1990 and now receives referrals from more than a hundred churches in the tristate area as a financially independent ministry. After the attacks of September 11, 2001, Redeemer Counseling became a counseling resource for the whole city.

Currently, Redeemer Counseling has more than fifty staff, coming from diverse backgrounds and training but united in love for God. They are biblically grounded and clinically trained. The staff serves hundreds of individuals, couples, and families, providing more than twenty thousand sessions each year. We offer professional counseling care that connects the truth of the gospel with clinical excellence.

In 2011, after experiencing double-digit growth each year, Redeemer Counseling embraced the mission to take its gospel-centered counseling care and influence individual hearts, churches, and the field of psychology. Since then we have been seeking to influence these spheres through counseling services, training, and research.

In the past few years, Redeemer Counseling has also become a training resource. Since the start of the COVID-19 pandemic, Redeemer Counseling took what its counselors have learned in the last three decades of ministry to more actively train other churches and ministries in the greater New York City area. More than twenty-five churches have partnered with Redeemer Counseling to care for their congregants through sponsorship of counseling sessions, hosting workshops, and offering training for their pastors and ministry leaders.

The following are a few resources that may be of interest to you:

- **REDEEMER COUNSELING UPDATES** is our quarterly newsletter for anyone who would like to know more about RCS and receive gospel-centered mental health and wellness tips.
- **COUNSELING TOOLKIT** is a resource for pastors, caregivers, and counselors. Each month we provide a skills-based counseling tool.
- **FELLOWS PROGRAM** is a nine-month counseling training program to help equip pastors and ministry leaders in their work of pastoral care.

To access these resources and find out more about our counseling services, training, and research, please visit our website: https://redeemercounseling.com.

# NOTES

## CHAPTER 1: THE REAL PROBLEM AND THE ULTIMATE SOLUTION

1. This often-used phrase by Timothy Keller was derived from Jack Miller's "Cheer up! You're a worse sinner than you ever dared imagine, and you're more loved than you ever dared hope."

2. Judy Cha, "The Essence of God Image Change in Psychotherapy from the Client's Perspective" (PhD diss., Eastern University, 2016).

## CHAPTER 2: OUR LOST IDENTITY AND THE EXPERIENCE OF SHAME

1. John M. Gottman and Nan Silver, *The Seven Principles for Making Marriage Work: A Practical Guide from the Country's Foremost Relationship Expert* (New York: Harmony Books, 1999).

2. For more on attachment theory, see Mary D. S. Ainsworth, "Attachments across the Life Span," *Bulletin of the New York Academy of Medicine* 61, no. 9 (1985): 792–812, PMCID: PMC1911889; and John Bowlby, *Attachment and Loss*, 3 vols. (New York: Basic Books, 1969–80).

## CHAPTER 3: WOUNDS THAT SHAPE WHO WE ARE

1. In psychology these are known as implicit relational representations (IRR).

2. In psychology these are referred to as adverse childhood experiences (ACEs). The original ACE study was conducted at Kaiser Permanente from 1995 to 1997. More than seventeen thousand patients receiving physical exams completed confidential surveys regarding their childhood experiences and current health status and behaviors. More detailed information about the study can be found in Vincent J. Felitti, Robert F. Anda, Dale Nordenberg, et al., "Relationship of Childhood Abuse and Household Dysfunction to Many of the Leading Causes of Death in Adults. The Adverse Childhood Experiences (ACE) Study," American Journal of Preventive Medicine, 14, no. 4 (May 1998): 245–58, https://doi.org/10.1016/s0749-3797 (98)00017-8. Please note: the original CDC-Kaiser data set is not available to the public.

3. Bruce D. Perry and Oprah Winfrey, *What Happened to You? Conversations on Trauma, Resilience, and Healing* (New York: Flatiron Books, 2021), ch. 5.

4. Perry, chs. 2 and 3.

5. Perry, 58, 92.

## CHAPTER 4: WAYS WE PROTECT OURSELVES AND ASSERT AN IDENTITY

1. Naomi I. Eisenberger, Matthew D. Lieberman, and Kipling D. Williams, "Does Rejection Hurt? An FMRI Study of Social Exclusion," *Science* 302, no. 5643 (October 2003): 290–92, doi:10.1126/science.1089134.

2. See Timothy Keller, *Counterfeit Gods: The Empty Promises of Money, Sex, and Power, and the Only Hope That Matters* (New York: Dutton, 2009). Keller's book masterfully describes how our hearts seek things besides

God to save us, and in many ways the book you are reading seeks to answer the question, *How do we escape this predicament?*

3. Keller, 64–66.

## CHAPTER 5: MORE THAN JUST "KNOWING" THE GOSPEL

1. Timothy Wilson, *Strangers to Ourselves: Discovering the Adaptive Unconscious* (Cambridge, MA: Harvard University Press, 2002).

2. Bruce D. Perry and Oprah Winfrey, *What Happened to You? Conversations on Trauma, Resilience, and Healing* (New York: Flatiron Books, 2021), 190.

3. Chris Fraley, David Fazzair, George Bonanno, and Sharon Dekel, "Attachment and Psychological Adaptation in High Exposure Survivors of the September 11th Attack on the World Trade Center," *Personality and Social Psychology Bulletin* 32 (2006): 538–51.

## CHAPTER 7: USING THE IMAGINATION TO ENCOUNTER GOD

1. See Glendon L. Moriarty and Louis Hoffman, eds., *God Image Handbook: For Spiritual Counseling and Psychotherapy* (Binghamton, NY: Haworth Pastoral Press, 2007).

2. For more details about the empirical results that support this framework, please refer to chapter 4 of P. Scott Richards, G. E. Kawika Allen, and Daniel K Judd, *Handbook of Spiritually Integrated Psychotherapies* (Washington, DC: American Psychological Association, 2023).

3. See Daniel J. Siegel, *The Developing Mind: How Relationships and the Brain Interact to Shape Who We Are*, 2nd ed. (New York: Guilford Press, 2012).

4. See Timothy and Kathy Keller, "Cultivating a Healthy

Marriage," April 1, 2005, *Gospel in Life*, produced by Redeemer Presbyterian Church, https://gospelinlife.com /downloads/cultivating-a-healthy-marriage-part-1-lecture -4656/.

## CHAPTER 9: CONNECTING WITH OTHERS

1. Maya Angelou, Quotes, Goodreads, accessed March 13, 2023, https://www.goodreads.com/quotes/5934-i-ve-learned -that-people-will-forget-what-you-said-people.
2. Julianne Holt-Lunstad, Timothy B. Smith, and J. Bradley Layton, "Social Relationships and Mortality Risk: A Meta-Analytic Review," *PLOS Medicine* 7, no. 7 (July 2010), https://doi.org/10.1371/journal.pmed.1000316.
3. Bruce D. Perry and Oprah Winfrey, *What Happened to You? Conversations on Trauma, Resilience, and Healing* (New York: Flatiron Books, 2021); Bessel van der Kolk, *The Body Keeps the Score: Brain, Mind, and Body in the Healing of Trauma* (New York: Penguin, 2014); and Angela Sweeney, Beth Filson, Angela Kennedy, et al., "A Paradigm Shift: Relationship in Trauma-Informed Mental Health Services," *BJPsych Advances* 24, no. 5 (September 2018): 319–33, https://doi.org/10.1192/bja.2018.29.
4. See Brené Brown, "The Power of Vulnerability," TED Talks, June 1, 2010, https://brenebrown.com/videos/ted-talk-the -power-of-vulnerability/.

## CHAPTER 10: DEEPLY CONNECTING WITH GOD

1. Todd W. Hall, Annie Fujikawa, Sarah R. Halcrow, et al., "Attachment to God and Implicit Spirituality: Clarifying Correspondence and Compensation Models," *Journal of Psychology and Theology* 37 (2009): 227–42.
2. Timothy Keller, "Gospel Identity," lecture, Gospel Identity Conference, November 18, 2017, Salvation Army

Auditorium, New York, https://gospelinlife.com/downloads
/gospel-identity/.

3. John Gottman, *The Science of Trust: Emotional
Attunement for Couples* (New York: Norton, 2011), 197.

4. See "Research," Johns Hopkins Medicine: Center for Music
& Medicine, 2022, https://www.hopkinsmedicine.org
/center-for-music-and-medicine/research.html; also Birthe K.
Flo, Anna Maria Matziorinis, Stavros Skouras, et al. "Study
Protocol for the Alzheimer and Music Therapy Study:
An RCT to Compare the Efficacy of Music Therapy and
Physical Activity on Brain Plasticity, Depressive Symptoms,
and Cognitive Decline, in a Population with and at Risk for
Alzheimer's Disease," *PLOS ONE* 17 (6), https://doi.org/10
.1371/journal.pone.0270682.

5. Hugh Hudson, dir., *Chariots of Fire*, Enigma Productions,
1981.